The Pollster's Dilemma

The Binomial Distribution and the Central Limit Theorem

Teacher's Guide

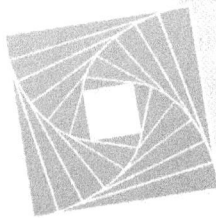

This material is based upon work supported by the National Science Foundation under award numbers ESI-9255262, ESI-0137805, and ESI-0627821. Any opinions, findings, and conclusions or recommendations expressed in this publication are those of the authors and do not necessarily reflect the views of the National Science Foundation.

Key Curriculum
1150 65th Street
Emeryville, California 94608
email: editorial@keypress.com
www.keycurriculum.com

First Edition Authors

Dan Fendel, Diane Resek, Lynne Alper, and Sherry Fraser

Contributors to the Second Edition

Sherry Fraser, Jean Klanica, Brian Lawler, Eric Robinson, Lew Romagnano, Rick Marks, Dan Brutlag, Alan Olds, Mike Bryant, Jeri P. Philbrick, Lori Green, Matt Bremer, Margaret DeArmond

Editor

Mali Apple

Editorial Assistant

Emily Reed

Professional Reviewer

Rick Marks, Sonoma State University

Math Checker

Carrie Gongaware

Production Editor

Andrew Jones

Production Director

Christine Osborne

Executive Editor

Josephine Noah

Mathematics Product Manager

Elizabeth DeCarli

Publisher

Steven Rasmussen

Contents

Introduction

Activity Notes

Introduction

The Pollster's Dilemma Unit Overview

Intent

In this unit, students explore how sample size is related to confidence in polling results.

Mathematics

The main concepts and skills that students will encounter and practice during the unit are summarized below.

General Sampling Concepts
- Establishing methods of good polling, including random sampling
- Using sampling from a known population to analyze the reliability of samples
- Distinguishing between sampling with replacement and sampling without replacement, and comparing the two methods
- Using the terminology *true proportion* and *sample proportion*
- Identifying simplifying assumptions in analyzing sampling

Specific Results on Sampling with Replacement
- Making probability bar graphs for various distributions
- Developing the concept of a theoretical distribution for sampling results from a given population
- Using combinatorial coefficients to find the theoretical distribution of poll results for polls of various sizes
- Generalizing that sampling results fit a binomial distribution

The Central Limit Theorem and the Normal Distribution
- Seeing intuitively that as poll size increases, the distribution of sample proportions becomes approximately normal
- Reviewing the concept of normal distribution
- Using estimates of areas to understand the normal distribution table
- Applying the central limit theorem for the case of binomial distributions

Mean and Standard Deviation
- Reviewing the steps for computation of standard deviation
- Seeing that the "large number of trials" method for computing mean and standard deviation is independent of the number of trials
- Extending the concepts of mean and standard deviation from sets of data to probability distributions
- Defining the concept of variance

- Finding formulas for the mean and standard deviation of the distribution of poll results in terms of the poll size and the true proportion
- Deciding what to use for σ if the true proportion is unknown, and finding the maximum value of σ for polling problems

Confidence Levels and Margin of Error
- Using the terminology *confidence level, confidence interval,* and *margin of error*
- Seeing how poll size affects the standard deviation of poll results
- Establishing confidence intervals in terms of sample proportions and standard deviation
- Seeing how the term *margin of error* is commonly used in news reporting
- Estimating the size of a poll based on the reported margin of error

Progression

The central limit theorem is the cornerstone of this unit on sampling. Through a variety of situations, students look at the process of sampling, with a special focus on how the size of the sample affects the variation in sample results.

The opening problem concerns an election poll that shows 53% of the voters favoring a particular candidate. The key question is this: **How confident should the candidate be about her lead, based on this poll?**

Students begin studying this question through an experimental sampling activity, which demonstrates that different polls from the same population can give different results. Students also learn the distinction between sampling with and without replacement.

Students see that for any given sampling scenario, there is a theoretical probability distribution for the results of the sample. For instance, they look at the case of a 3-person sample, taken with replacement, from a population that is 60% in favor of a given candidate. They find the probability that the sample is 100% for the candidate, the probability that the sample is $66\frac{2}{3}$% for the candidate, and so on. They review ideas from the Year 3 unit *Pennant Fever* about how to find such probabilities in general, and they realize that the results fit a binomial distribution.

Next, students look at probability bar graphs for samples of different sizes for a given overall population. They see that as sample size increases, there is less variation among different samples and the theoretical probability distribution increasingly resembles a normal distribution. They learn that the central limit theorem confirms this observation.

Students see that the amount of variation from one poll to another (taken from the same population) is related to the concept of standard deviation. They worked with this concept in the Year 1 unit *The Pit and the Pendulum* in terms of a set of data. Through a "wheel of fortune" problem and other situations, they now see how to extend standard deviation from sets of data to situations defined by probabilities.

In particular, students find the mean and variance in the number of "yes" votes for small polls from a specific overall population and use patterns from this information to get the formula $\sqrt{np(1-p)}$ for the standard deviation in the *number* of "yes" votes. Then, using algebra, they convert this formula to the formula $\sqrt{\dfrac{p(1-p)}{n}}$ for the standard deviation in the *proportion* of "yes" votes.

Next, students work on problems to learn how to use standard deviation and the approximately normal distribution of sample proportions to estimate the true proportion of support for a candidate in an overall population. This work includes the concepts of confidence interval and margin of error, and demonstrates clearly to students that standard deviation is the key to understanding the central unit problem.

Along the way to solving the unit problem, students confront the issue that their standard deviation and confidence intervals for a poll are expressed in terms of p (the true proportion), yet the goal of the poll is to find p. This leads to the principle that the cautious approach for a pollster is to use the "worst-case scenario": to find the largest possible value for the standard deviation. Students discover that this occurs when $p = .5$, that is, when the population is evenly divided.

In addition to solving the unit problem and applying the ideas to a central problem from the Year 2 unit *Is There Really a Difference?*, students work in pairs on a sampling project for a question of their own, writing reports and making presentations that involve choosing a sample size and applying the unit's main concepts.

What's a Pollster to Think?: Introducing the central unit problem and exploring sampling variation experimentally

Polls and "Pennant Fever": Developing the theoretical probability distribution for polls of different sizes using sampling with replacement

Normal Distributions Revisited: Reviewing and extending ideas about the normal distribution

Means and Standard Deviations: Finding the mean and standard deviation for the normal distribution that approximates polling results

A Matter of Confidence: Planning the unit polling project; defining and using the concepts of confidence level, confidence interval, and margin of error

Putting It Together: Applying concepts from the unit to a Year 2 problem and to the central unit problem, carrying out the unit polling project and making project presentations, completing assessments, and summing up

Pacing Guides

50-minute Pacing Guide (26 days)

Day	Activity	In-Class Time Estimate
	What's a Pollster to Think?	0
1	*The Pollster's Dilemma*	40
	Introduce: *POW 5: The King's Switches*	10
	Homework: *No Bias Allowed!*	0
2	Discussion: *No Bias Allowed*	15
	Sampling Seniors	30
	Homework: *"Pennant Fever" Reflection*	5
3	Discussion: *"Pennant Fever" Reflection*	20
	Sampling Seniors (continued)	30
	Homework: *Bags of Marbles and Bowls of Ice Cream*	0
4	Verify POW 5 answers for $n = 3$ and $n = 4$	5
	Discussion: *Bags of Marbles and Bowls of Ice Cream*	10
	Polls and Pennant Fever	0
	The Theory of Three-Person Polls	35
	Homework: *Graphs of the Theory*	0
5	Discussion: *Graphs of the Theory*	10
	The Theory of Polls	40
	Homework: *Civics in Action*	0
6	Discussion: *Civics in Action*	10
	Normal Distributions Revisited	0
	Reference: *The Central Limit Theorem*	20
	Deviations of Swinging	20
	Homework: *Means and More in Middletown*	0
7	Presentations and discussion: *POW 5: The King's Switches*	15
	Discussion: *Means and More in Middletown*	10
	Graphing Distributions	25

	Homework: *Gifts Aren't Always Free*	0
8	Discussion: *Gifts Aren't Always Free*	10
	Normal Areas	25
	Reference: *The Normal Table*	15
	Homework: *More Middletown Musings*	0
9	Discussion: *More Middletown Musings*	15
	Back to the Circus	35
	Homework: *Gaps in the Table*	0
10	Discussion: *Gaps in the Table*	10
	A Normal Poll	40
	Homework: *A Plus for the Community*	0
11	Discussion: *A Plus for the Community*	15
	Means and Standard Deviations	0
	Reference: *Mean and Standard Deviation for Probability Distributions*	35
	Homework: *A Distribution Example*	0
12	Discussion: *A Distribution Example*	10
	The Search Is On!	40
	Homework: *Why Is That Batter Sneezing?*	0
13	Discussion: *Why Is That Batter Sneezing?*	10
	The Search Is On! (continued)	40
	Homework: *Putting Your Formulas to Work*	0
14	Discussion: *Putting Your Formulas to Work*	10
	From Numbers to Proportions	40
	Homework: *Is Twice as Many Twice as Good?*	0
15	Discussion: *Is Twice as Many Twice as Good?*	10
	A Matter of Confidence	0
	Different p, Different σ	30
	Introduce: *Let's Vote on It!*	10
	Homework: *Project Topics and Random Polls*	0
16	*Different p, Different σ* (continued)	10

	Discussion: *Project Topics and Random Polls*	40
	Homework: *Mean, Median, and Mode*	0
17	Discussion: *Mean, Median, and Mode*	10
	The Worst-Case Scenario	40
	Homework: *A Teaching Dilemma*	0
18	Discussion: *A Teaching Dilemma*	10
	What Does It Mean?	40
	Homework: *Confidence and Clarabell*	0
19	Discussion: *Confidence and Clarabell*	10
	Polling Puzzles	35
	Homework: *How Big?*	5
20	Discussion: *How Big?*	10
	Putting It Together	0
	Roberto and the Coin	35
	Homework: *How Much Better Is Bigger?*	5
21	Discussion: *How Much Better Is Bigger?*	10
	"The Pollster's Dilemma" Revisited	40
	Homework: *Final Data Collection*	0
22	*Let's Vote on It!* (partners work in class)	50
	Homework: *"The Pollster's Dilemma" Portfolio*	0
23	Presentations: *Let's Vote on It!*	50
24	Presentations: *Let's Vote on It!* (continued)	50
25	In-Class Assessment	40
	Homework: Take-Home Assessment	10
26	Exam Discussion	40
	Unit Reflection	10

90-minute Pacing Guide (18 days)

Day	Activity	In-Class Time Estimate
	What's a Pollster to Think?	0
1	*The Pollster's Dilemma*	40
	Introduce: *POW 5: The King's Switches*	10
	No Bias Allowed!	35
	Homework: *"Pennant Fever" Reflection*	5
2	Discussion: *"Pennant Fever" Reflection*	20
	Sampling Seniors	70
	Homework: *Bags of Marbles and Bowls of Ice Cream*	0
3	Verify POW 5 answers for $n = 3$ and $n = 4$	5
	Discussion: *Bags of Marbles and Bowls of Ice Cream*	10
	Polls and Pennant Fever	0
	The Theory of Three-Person Polls	35
	Graphs of the Theory	40
4	*The Theory of Polls*	40
	Civics in Action	30
	Normal Distributions Revisited	0
	Reference: The Central Limit Theorem	20
	Homework: *Deviations of Swinging*	0
5	*Reference: The Central Limit Theorem* (continued)	10
	Means and More in Middletown	45
	Graphing Distributions	35
	Homework: *Gifts Aren't Always Free*	0
6	Discussion: *Gifts Aren't Always Free*	10
	Presentations and discussion: *POW 5: The King's Switches*	20
	Normal Areas	40
	Reference: The Normal Table	20
	Homework: *More Middletown Musings*	0
7	Discussion: *More Middletown Musings*	15

	How Big?	40
	Putting It Together	0
	Roberto and the Coin	35
	Homework: *How Much Better Is Bigger?*	5
15	Discussion: *How Much Better Is Bigger?*	10
	Roberto and the Coin (continued)	10
	"The Pollster's Dilemma" Revisited	40
	"The Pollster's Dilemma" Portfolio	30
	Homework: *Final Data Collection*	0
16	*"The Pollster's Dilemma" Portfolio* (continued)	30
	Let's Vote on It! (partners work in class)	60
17	Presentations: *Let's Vote on It!*	45
	In-Class Assessment	40
	Homework: Take-Home Assessment	5
18	Exam Discussion	35
	Presentations: *Let's Vote on It!* (continued)	45
	Unit Reflection	10

Materials and Supplies

All IMP classrooms should have a set of standard supplies, described in the section "Materials and Supplies for the IMP Classroom" in A Guide to IMP. You'll also find a comprehensive list of materials needed for all Year 4 units in the section "Materials and Supplies for Year 4" in the Year 4 Teacher's Guide general resources.

Listed here are the supplies needed for this unit. Also available are general and activity-specific blackline masters, for transparencies or for student worksheets, in the "Blackline Masters" section in The Diver Returns Unit Resources.

More About Supplies

Graph paper is a standard supply for IMP classrooms. Blackline masters of 1-Centimeter Graph Paper, 1/4-Inch Graph Paper, and 1-inch Graph Paper are provided, for you to make copies and transparencies.

Assessing Progress

The Pollster's Dilemma concludes with two formal unit assessments. In addition, there are many opportunities for more informal, ongoing assessments throughout the unit. For more information about assessment and grading, including general information about the end-of-unit assessments and how to use them, consult *A Guide to IMP*.

End-of-Unit Assessments

This unit concludes with in-class and take-home assessments. The in-class assessment is intentionally short so that time pressures will not affect student performance. Students may use graphing calculators and their notes from previous work when they take the assessments. You can download unit assessments from the *The Pollster's Dilemma* Unit Resources.

Also included is a final assessment for the first semester of Year 4, suitable for schools using a traditional semester schedule. This assessment is designed on the assumption that your class will have completed *The Diver Returns*, *The World of Functions*, and up through *A Plus for the Community* of *The Pollster's Dilemma*. This semester assessment is not intended to be a comprehensive test of the material in these units, but focuses instead on some essential ideas. We recommend that you give students two hours for the assessment so they can complete it without time pressure and that you allow them to use calculators as well as to have access to their textbooks, notes, and portfolios.

Ongoing Assessment

One of the primary tasks of the classroom teacher is to assess student learning. Although the assigning of course grades may be part of this process, assessment more broadly includes the daily work of determining how well students understand key ideas and what level of achievement they have attained on key skills, in order to provide the best possible ongoing instructional program for them.

Students' written and oral work provides many opportunities for teachers to gather this information. We make some recommendations here of activities to monitor especially carefully that will give you insight into student progress.

- *Graphs of the Theory*
- *Gifts Aren't Always Free*
- *A Normal Poll*
- *The Search Is On!*
- *What Does It Mean?*
- *"The Pollster's Dilemma" Revisited*

Discussion of Unit Assessments

Have students volunteer to explain their work on each of the problems. Encourage questions and alternate explanations from other students.

In-Class Assessment

For Question 1, students should combine the formula $\sigma = \sqrt{\dfrac{p(1-p)}{n}}$ with the fact that $2\sigma = .04$ (because a 95% confidence level represents the interval of width 2σ around the mean, and the margin of error is .04). Using the worst-case scenario (that is, considering $p = .5$, which requires the largest value for n), this gives the equation

$$2 \cdot \sqrt{\frac{.5 \cdot .5}{n}} = .04$$

This simplifies to $\dfrac{1}{\sqrt{n}} = .04$, which yields $n = 625$.

For Question 2a, students should see that as the sample size increases, the standard deviation of the sample proportion decreases. They should be able to explain this intuitively, perhaps saying there should be less variation in the sample proportion among large polls than among small polls. They should also use the formula $\sigma = \sqrt{\dfrac{p(1-p)}{n}}$ to show that σ decreases as n increases.

For Question 2b, students should see intuitively that for a given poll size, being more confident that the true proportion is within the margin of error simply requires a larger margin of error. In terms of the procedure for finding the margin of error, they should explain that a larger confidence level corresponds to a larger z-value. But the margin of error is simply the product of the z-value and the standard deviation, and the standard deviation is unchanged because the poll size is fixed, so increasing the z-value leads to a larger margin of error.

Take-Home Assessment

Question 1 is similar to Question 1 of *The Theory of Polls*, except that here students are considering the case $p = .8$. The probability bar graph below shows the results. This graph is also included on a blackline master.

Distribution of 5-person polls with
true proportion = 80%

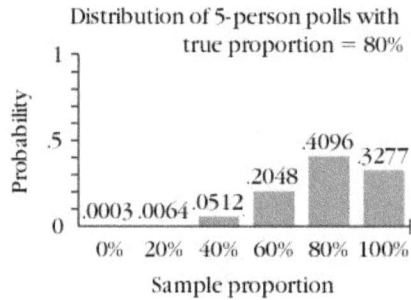

Question 2 gives students an opportunity to show their understanding of a variety of concepts. Here are some conclusions you might get:

- The poll size is 300.
- The sample proportion is 53.3% (or .533).
- The standard deviation for polls of this size is $\dfrac{.5}{\sqrt{300}}$, or approximately .029.
- The margin of error (using a 95% confidence level) is approximately 5.7%.
- The 95% confidence interval is approximately from 47.6% to 59.1%.
- Coretta is leading if the true proportion is at least equal to the value roughly 1.15 standard deviations below the sample proportion.
- Coretta can be roughly 87.6% confident that she is leading.

Rounding at different stages may produce some variations among students' answers.

Supplemental Activities

The unit contains a variety of activities at the end of the student pages that you can use to supplement the regular unit material. These activities fall roughly into two categories.

Reinforcements increase students' understanding and comfort with concepts, techniques, and methods that are discussed in class and are central to the unit.

Extensions allow students to explore ideas beyond those presented in the unit, including generalizations and abstractions of ideas.

The supplemental activities are presented in the teacher's guide and the student book in the approximate sequence in which you might use them. Below are specific recommendations about how each activity might work within the unit. You may wish to use some of these activities, especially the later ones, after the unit is completed.

***What Is Random?* (reinforcement or extension)** This activity can be used at any point in the unit. However, because the concept of randomness is central to the unit, it makes sense to use this within the first week or so.

***Random Number Generators* (extension)** This activity can also be used at any point in the unit.

***The Tack or the Coin?* (reinforcement)** This activity can be used as a follow-up to *Sampling Seniors.* In that activity, students look at how sampling results from a known population vary. In this activity, students use results from an experiment to predict what will happen in a future experiment. If students work on this activity late in the unit, you might ask them to provide a confidence interval for their estimate of how often the tack lands point up.

***Three-Person Races* (extension)** This activity is a natural follow-up to students' work with *The Theory of Polls.* However, you may want to wait until the binomial distribution has been summarized formally in the review of the reference pages *The Central Limit Theorem* before assigning this activity.

***Generalizing Linear Interpolation* (extension)** This activity asks students to generalize the ideas presented in *Gaps in the Table* and is a good follow-up to that activity.

***Another View of the Central Limit Theorem* (reinforcement or extension)** This activity provides students with a chance to see the central limit theorem in a context somewhat more general than the polling situations that are the focus of this unit. This activity also involves mean and standard deviation and is probably best used after *The Search Is On!*

It's the News (**reinforcement**) This activity gives students another opportunity to think about how polling is reported in the media. It can be used after students have an understanding of the term *margin of error,* such as after *The Worst-Case Scenario.*

What's a Pollster to Think?

Intent

These activities introduce the central unit question.

Mathematics

The central question for this unit is, "How is our trust in a sample affected by the sample size?" In these activities, students consider the importance of the random sample and observe the variation that can occur in sample results. They learn to construct a probability bar graph that represents a simple theoretical probability distribution. In preparation for studying more complex probability distributions, they review the use of combinatorial coefficients to find probabilities.

Progression

The Pollster's Dilemma introduces the central unit question regarding polling. In *No Bias Allowed!* students see the importance of avoiding bias through random samples. *Sampling Seniors* is a class experiment that highlights the variation that is possible in polling results and leads into consideration of theoretical probability distributions. As sample sizes increase, the construction of such probability distributions involves the use of combinatorial coefficients, which are reviewed in *"Pennant Fever" Reflection* and *Bags of Marbles and Bowls of Ice Cream*.

The Pollster's Dilemma
No Bias Allowed!
POW 5: The King's Switches
Sampling Seniors
Pennant Fever Reflection
Bags of Marbles and Bowls of Ice Cream

The Pollster's Dilemma

Intent

This activity introduces the central unit question and suggests a plan for exploring it.

Mathematics

The class discusses the meaning of poll results and begins to develop principles of good polling. The discussion brings out the importance of randomness and the role of sample size.

Progression

In an optional introduction to this unit, the class reviews news stories that describe poll results and discuss what the results really mean. After an introduction to the activity, students explore the questions. The subsequent discussion clarifies the importance of randomness in polling and reveals that the role of sample size will be central to the unit. Simplifying assumptions that will be used in the unit are summarized. The discussion concludes by outlining the general plan for this unit: using sampling from a known population to analyze the reliability of samples.

Approximate Time

40 minutes

Classroom Organization

Small groups, preceded and followed by whole-class discussion

Materials

Optional: One or more news stories about polls, perhaps using the phrase *margin of error*

Doing the Activity

One nice way to introduce the unit is to give each group a news story from a newspaper, magazine, or the Internet describing the results of a poll. (You don't need a different story for every group, although some variety would be good.) After a few minutes, have members of each group share what information was provided about the poll and give their interpretations of the results. If the story uses such terminology as *confidence level* or *margin of error,* you might have students speculate about what the terms mean.

Then, have the class read the description of the situation in the central unit problem, *The Pollster's Dilemma,* or have volunteers read it aloud.

If the class didn't discuss examples of polls from news sources, ask students what they know about polls. **What is a poll? What is the purpose of conducting a poll?** In particular, bring out that polls represent samples taken from some larger population and that they are often used to form the basis for a decision about some future action.

Then let students work on the questions. Question 1 will give them a straightforward introduction to the topic before they get into the more open-ended questions.

Discussing and Debriefing the Activity

The purpose of this discussion is to identify important questions about polls and their significance, not to provide specific answers. As the discussion proceeds, identify issues that will be central to the unit and those that will be dealt with only slightly or not at all.

Over the course of the unit, students will review or be introduced to many terms. We recommend that you create a poster listing new or important terms and definitions or have students create individual lists.

For Question 1, ask a volunteer to report the actual numbers of voters for and against Coretta and another to explain how many switched votes it would take to change the outcome. Because there are 265 voters for and 235 against, this means that if the poll had happened to pick "no" voters in place of 15 of the "yes" voters, the poll would have indicated a tie.

Question 1b essentially assumes that all non-"yes" votes are actually votes *against* Coretta and that Coretta must garner a majority of votes to win the election. Some vote-counting schemes do not fit this model. If students raise this issue, help them make an appropriate simplifying assumption.

Based on the answer to Question 1b, students may think the poll doesn't mean a whole lot. That is, they may feel that because a switch of only 15 votes would lead to a tie, Coretta cannot be very secure about her situation.

Let students know that one goal of the unit will be to investigate the significance of the size of the margin in a poll. In particular, is it appropriate to describe the number of switched votes needed as "only" 15?

About all the poll result means for sure is exactly what it says—that 53% of the 500 people polled said they intend to vote for Coretta. Be sure students realize that this does not mean that 53% of all eligible voters support Coretta.

For Question 3, two main issues will likely arise, in terms of either information students want about the current poll or suggestions for future polls:

- The people polled should be selected at random.
- The sample should be "large enough."

Randomness

Students will probably want to know things like how the poll was taken and whether the people polled were representative of the overall city population. The issue of randomness is an important one, so be sure to review the meaning of the term **random**.

What does *random* mean? Make sure students know that a random sample is one in which each voter has an equal chance of being selected. This will ensure the sample is not automatically biased toward particular points of view that are not representative of the population as a whole. (The use of the word **bias** in polling is discussed in *No Bias Allowed!*)

Students should know from previous work that even a random sample will not necessarily come out exactly like the overall population, just as a fair coin won't necessarily come out heads exactly half the time in a given set of flips. One of the main tasks for students in this unit is to determine how much variation actually occurs in random samples of various sizes.

What are some procedures that might lead to polls that are not random? Suggest one or two of these examples if students need help getting started:

- Asking voters outside an expensive mall. (This would overrepresent wealthier people.)
- Picking random numbers from a phone book. (This would underrepresent people with no phone or unlisted numbers.)
- Asking people at a bus stop. (This would include only people who ride public transportation, who might tend to be less wealthy than average.)

Students should see that it is very difficult to get an unbiased sample of voters. *No Bias Allowed!* continues the discussion of this issue.

You may want to mention that randomness is a theoretical concept and that no practical scheme can be perfectly random. Tell students that in this unit, the mathematical analysis will be based on the assumption that the selection of participants in a poll is random. (This is one of several assumptions that will be discussed later today.)

Sample Size

If the issue of sample size didn't come up in the discussion of Question 2, be sure to raise it now.

Some students may believe that a poll of 500 people is not large enough to give meaningful results about a city with 400,000 voters. If so, ask what sample size they would consider "big enough." Don't be surprised if they pick very large sample sizes or say, "You can't know for sure unless you ask everybody." Explain that exploring the significance of sample size will be an important component of this unit.

Tell the class that mathematicians often prefer the word *sample* as a synonym for "poll" in order to cover a broader class of situations. They also use the term *sample size* as an alternative to "poll size." The poll gives information about a sample of the population of eligible voters in the city.

Other Issues

Students may mention other issues that can complicate the polling process, such as these:

- Eligible voters don't all vote.
- People don't always tell pollsters their true opinions.
- Opinions might change before the election.
- There may be more than two candidates.

These and similar problems are important issues for professional pollsters and others who do surveys. Although the unit will not address such issues beyond today's discussion, the issues may come up in students' projects (see *Let's Vote on It!*). You may want to remind students of these issues occasionally so that they remain aware that the unit is dealing with a simplified version of a complex problem. One way pollsters deal with the first issue is to poll only those who are likely to vote (if they can figure out who those people are).

A good start toward handling the second issue is to make the poll confidential, though even anonymity may not guarantee honesty. An often-cited example concerns a telephone poll in which people were asked if they washed their hands after using a bathroom. Although 94% said yes, direct observations in public facilities showed that the actual rate is more like 68%.

Concerning the third issue, acknowledge that a poll near election time is generally a better predictor than a poll taken long before the election. But taking a poll right before an election leaves the candidate less time in which to make use of poll results.

About the fourth issue, tell students that the unit will not consider the case of more than two candidates, as the mathematics of polls that involve more than two choices is considerably more complicated. (This issue however, is raised in the supplemental activity *Three-Person Races*.)

A Summary of Simplifying Assumptions

Explain that many complex issues arise in the real world of polling, but that we will make several simplifying assumptions in this unit to make the problem manageable and to focus on certain mathematical ideas common to all polling problems. You will probably have already touched on the issues underlying most of these assumptions, but it is important to make them explicit.

Ask, **What assumptions do you think are important to make?** Have students make a list. Be sure to include the items listed here, bringing them up yourself if necessary.

- People in a poll are selected at random from the population of eligible voters.
- All eligible voters actually vote.
- Voters tell pollsters their real opinions.
- Voters do not change their opinions between the time of the poll and the actual election.
- The election is a 2-person race.
- There are no undecided voters.

Post these assumptions as a reminder to students as they work through the unit, leaving room to add other assumptions as the unit progresses.

The Central Unit Question

Ask, **What do you think the central question of the unit is?** Although students may have a variety of ideas, focus on Coretta's desire to know whether she will win the election.

What poll results would *guarantee* that Coretta is leading when the poll is taken? Students should see that to be completely certain, they would need a poll showing at least 200,001 people supporting Coretta. This should help direct the discussion to the issue of *confidence.* Essentially, the main question of the unit is this:

> **Based on a particular poll, how confident can Coretta be that she will win?**

Tell students that the unit will focus on a particular aspect of this question, namely:

> **How much is our trust in a sample affected by the sample size?**

The formal term *confidence level* will be introduced in *Different p, Different σ*.

Developing a General Plan

Ask, **How might you begin exploring these central questions?** Let students discuss the issues for a few minutes in their groups, and then have them share ideas.

The goal is to elicit the idea of experimenting with polls from a known population (that is, a population in which the proportion supporting the candidate is known) to see what happens with such polls. Students should then recognize that they will have to try different poll sizes to see how the "amount of confidence" varies with poll size.

In a sense, the unit begins by working backward. Students will assume they know the proportion supporting the candidate (the *true proportion*) and will examine the probability of getting a particular poll result (the *sample proportion*). Once they complete this analysis, they will see how to solve the "real" polling problem—that is, how to estimate the true proportion based on knowing the sample proportion.

Key Questions

What is a poll? What is the purpose of conducting a poll?
What does *random* mean?
What are some procedures that might lead to polls that are not random?
What assumptions do you think are important to make?
What do you think the central question of the unit is?
What poll results would *guarantee* that Coretta is leading when the poll is taken?
How might you begin exploring these central questions?

No Bias Allowed!

Intent

Students explore the issue of bias in a sample.

Mathematics

In this activity, students identify ways in which a sample may be biased. Avoiding bias through the use of random sampling is a big issue in sampling, but in the central unit problem, students assume they are working with a randomly selected sample. They will see this is a difficult, perhaps impossible, goal to achieve in practice. For their unit projects, they will simply try to select samples as randomly as possible (see *Project Topics and Random Polls*).

Progression

Students explain how each of several methods of choosing a sample might bias the results and then describe and discuss methods for choosing a random sample. The point of this discussion is to make students aware of the difficulty of avoiding bias and to help them develop good procedures for selecting samples for their unit projects.

Approximate Time

25 minutes for activity (at home or in class)
15 minutes for discussion

Classroom Organization

Individuals or small groups, followed by whole-class discussion

Doing the Activity

This activity requires no introduction.

Discussing and Debriefing the Activity

Question 1

Students should see that in this context, the word *sample* refers to the group of students that are polled. However, they may disagree about what the population is.

For instance, some students might say there are those who don't like proms and would not attend at any price, and that such students should not be part of the population. Others may associate "prom" with "senior prom" and think the population should be seniors. No consensus needs to be reached, but have students keep in mind that the designation of a specific group as the population may affect whether the sample is representative.

Question 2

Let students comment on each proposed method of choosing the sample. Here are some possible flaws:

- Question 2a: Perhaps only wealthier students drive to school.
- Question 2b: A group of students leaving together may be friends and tend to share a viewpoint or economic status.
- Question 2c: Students may not all be taking mathematics, or some courses may contain a disproportionate number of students with a particular opinion.

For Question 2a, one would expect that students in the group polled would be less concerned than the average student about the price of prom tickets. For Questions 2b and 2c, there is no predictable direction for the bias, but the proposed sample may not fairly represent the school.

Question 3

Ask volunteers to share their plans, and encourage constructive criticism from the other students. In evaluating plans, highlight the idea that the "representativeness" of a plan depends on what the defined population is.

Students may suggest something like, "Make a list of all students in the desired population and then pick people at random from the list." They may even propose using a random number generator. If so, you might mention that carrying out the polling for a group selected this way is more difficult than for the "flawed" methods described in the activity. Make students aware that pollsters have to deal with practical issues like finding the people in their sample.

Optional: Stratified Samples

Tell students that in an attempt to achieve representative samples, pollsters often use something more complex than pure random **sampling.** For example, election pollsters purposely take men and women in the same proportion in which they occur in the chosen population (whether that population is registered voters, or likely voters, or whatever). Similarly, they select a certain number from each economic group, from different regions, from urban versus rural versus suburban locales, and so on.

In effect, pollsters take many smaller samples from subpopulations and put them together proportionately into one larger group. This process, called *stratified sampling,* is based on the assumption that the variation within these smaller groups is less than the variation within the overall population. In other words, the assumption is that certain subpopulations will vote somewhat as a block. If this assumption is correct (and the subpopulations are chosen well), pollsters can get results of a particular reliability with a smaller sample than they would need using a purely random survey.

Supplemental Activities

***What Is Random?* (reinforcement or extension)** asks students to summarize what they have learned about the concept of randomness.

***Random Number Generators* (extension)** challenges students to investigate how a random number generator works.

POW 5: The King's Switches

Intent

Students investigate a complex problem and communicate the solution convincingly.

Mathematics

In this Problem of the Week, students explore recursion.

Progression

Several days after this POW is introduced, students are given an opportunity to check their findings for two specific cases to ensure they understand the situation. After about a week, several students present their findings, leading into a whole-class discussion.

Approximate Time

10 minutes for introduction
3 to 5 hours for activity (at home)
5 minutes for verifying partial solutions (on the third or fourth day)
15 to 20 minutes for presentations and discussion

Classroom Organization

Individuals, followed by presentations and whole-class discussion

Doing the Activity

A couple of days after assigning this POW, instruct students to have the numeric results for the cases $n = 3$ and $n = 4$ on the next day. (No proofs are expected yet.) On the following day, ask one or two students for their answers to these cases. The goal is to be sure students understand the rules for the switches and are on the right track in compiling a table of minimal values.

For $n = 3$, the minimum is 5 moves; for $n = 4$, it is 10 moves. If students got smaller values, they have made a mistake. You might suggest they go through their sequence of steps with a partner. If students got larger values, they are probably including unnecessary steps in the process. You might suggest they look for a more efficient method of deactivating the system.

On the day before the POW is due, choose three students to prepare presentations for the following day.

Discussing and Debriefing the Activity

You might have each presenter take one of the values 3, 4, or 5 for n and explain why his or her answer is the minimum number of moves possible.

The analysis becomes more interesting as n increases. For instance, for $n = 5$, the key insight is that to change switch 5, one must get the switches to these positions:

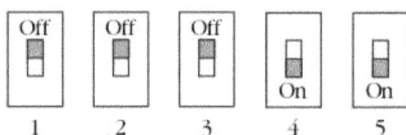

This requires changing the first three switches from on to off, which is the task for the case $n = 3$. In fact, for any value of n, the first stage of the task is to change the first $n - 2$ switches to off in order to change switch n.

This observation suggests the recursive nature of the problem. However, it's not easy to see how to proceed with the analysis in general. For instance, once switch 5 is turned off, the setup looks like this:

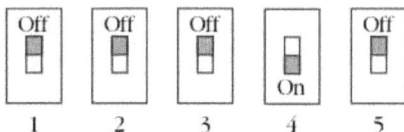

Changing switch 4 does not require "undoing" the first stage (that is, turning the first three switches back on), but instead requires getting to this situation:

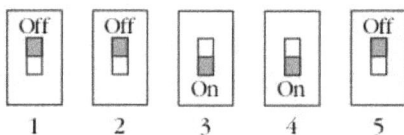

Once switch 4 is turned off, the last stage is to change the first three switches back to a sequence of three offs.

The General Problem

After discussing the specific cases $n = 3$, 4, and 5, let volunteers share ideas about the general problem. If they find enough correct rows for a table like this one, they may see a pattern among the *Out* values.

n	Number of moves needed
1	1
2	2
3	5
4	10
5	21

Specifically, they may notice that as n increases by 1, the number of moves needed either doubles or doubles and adds 1. For instance, from $n = 3$ to $n = 4$, the number of moves needed doubles, from 5 to 10. From $n = 4$ to $n = 5$, the number of moves needed goes from 10 to 21, which is 1 more than doubling.

As students explore this pattern, they are likely to see that the two rules alternate. You might suggest they introduce a notation such as a_n for the number of moves required for n switches and then represent the relationship in a recursive equation. Here is one way to express the relationship:

$$a_{n+1} = \begin{cases} 2a_n & \text{if } n \text{ is odd} \\ 2a_n + 1 & \text{if } n \text{ is even} \end{cases}$$

This recursion equation will allow students to extend the table easily, although it will not allow them to compute a_n directly for a large value of n. For instance, if they know that $a_5 = 21$, this equation tells them that $a_6 = 2 \cdot 21 = 42$ (because 5 is odd) and that $a_7 = 2 \cdot 42 + 1 = 85$ (because 6 is even). By this method, students can determine that $a_{10} = 682$.

A Closed Formula

It is possible to get a closed formula for a_n, although the formula is far from obvious. One clue is that even and odd values seem to behave differently, which suggests looking at the results separately. This table displays only odd values of n:

n	a_n
1	1
3	5
5	21
7	85
9	341

Examining successive differences shows that a_n increases by 4, then 16, then 64, and then 256. Because these differences are powers of 2, students might guess that the outputs themselves (the values of a_n) are related to powers of 2.

Students might then see that if they multiply a_n by 3 and then add 1, the result is 2^{n+1}. For instance, $3a_5 + 1 = 3 \cdot 21 + 1 = 64 = 2^6$. Working backward from this gives

$$a_n = \frac{2^{n+1} - 1}{3} \quad \text{when } n \text{ is odd}$$

A similar approach for even values of n gives

$$a_n = \frac{2^{n+1} - 2}{3} \quad \text{when } n \text{ is even}$$

Be sure students are aware they have not *proved* these formulas. (The proof is quite sophisticated.)

Sampling Seniors

Intent

Students use experimentation to investigate the results of sampling.

Mathematics

This activity is an open-ended opportunity for students to explore the results of polls of different sizes. The experiment will illustrate how varied the results of sampling can be. Students will develop the concept of a theoretical distribution for sampling results from a given population and use a probability graph to illustrate that distribution.

Progression

Groups use objects in a bag to experiment with taking samples of various sizes, with replacement, trying to see how small a sample can be while still giving a good idea of the population. They make a frequency bar graph of the results for each set of samples. The subsequent discussion introduces theoretical probability distributions and probability bar graphs.

Approximate Time

60 to 70 minutes

Classroom Organization

Small groups, followed by whole-class discussion

Materials

Large supply of *identical* objects in two colors (such as beans, marbles, color cubes, or tag-board squares) so each group has 90 of one color and 60 of the other
Paper bags (1 per group)
Optional: Transparency of *Sampling Seniors* blackline master

Doing the Activity

Have students read the activity, and then call on several students to state the sampling task clearly. Make sure students realize that for Questions 1 and 2, they need to do 20 polls of the same size, keep track of their results, and make a frequency bar graph of the results. If time allows, they can do additional sets of 20 polls using other sample sizes.

You might ask groups for suggestions about how they can organize their work efficiently. One idea is for two students to draw the objects from the bag and count the results while the other two record the data and make the frequency bar graph.

Choosing Sample Sizes

In *The Theory of Three-Person Polls*, students will look at the issue of sampling in a more structured way, examining theoretical results for 3-person polls. We suggest that you have at least one group collect data for 3-person polls in today's activity so you have some "real data" to compare with the theoretical results in that activity. You might also assign sample sizes such as 5, 8, 10, 12, and 15 to give a good balance between getting "good" results and not being too time-consuming.

If possible, have each group complete at least two sets of 20 polls. (If your class is small, you may want to allow time for each group to do more than two sets in order to get more results altogether.) If some groups seem to be working efficiently, have them try a large poll size (20 or more) and do 20 polls of that size.

Discussing and Debriefing the Activity

Ask a member of each group to share the group's frequency bar graphs. In particular, have each group state, for each set of 20 polls they did, how many of those polls show a majority favoring Cesar Chavez Center. Because the overall population prefers Cesar Chavez Center, one might consider a poll to be "successful" if it reflects the choice of the majority.

Have groups that considered a sample size of 3 save their results for comparison with the theoretical results they will obtain in *The Theory of Three-Person Polls*. (Save the number of times each outcome occurred, not just the number of polls favoring Cesar Chavez Center.)

Question 4

Let volunteers share any general conclusions they reached for Question 4. Bring out that larger polls tend to give results that are closer to the overall population. However, as with polling for the central unit problem, students should see that the only way to obtain absolute certainty is to continue until they have at least 76 of the 150 students voting for a particular site. The key issue here is balancing the desire for greater certainty with the practical need to limit the sample size.

Tell students that a key component of this unit is determining the probability of getting each possible result from a poll of a given size. Introduce the term **probability distribution** (also called *theoretical probability distribution* or *theoretical distribution*) for this set of probabilities. Emphasize that these probabilities depend on both the population from which the sample is taken and on the sample size. Students will have to take both factors into account.

Ask students, How might you find these theoretical probabilities? One likely response is that they could do the experiment many more times and see what happens. Tell them they will be learning a more theoretical approach that applies to all sizes and all populations.

A One-Person Poll Example

To clarify the meaning of the phrase *probability distribution,* go over the case of a 1-person poll. First ask, What might the result be for a 1-person poll? Students should see there are only two possible outcomes: the poll will show either one vote or no votes in favor of using Cesar Chavez Center.

What is the probability of each possible result? Students should be able to explain that the probability of getting one vote for Cesar Chavez Center is $\frac{90}{150}$ and the probability of getting no votes is $\frac{60}{150}$. Therefore, for a 1-person poll, the probability distribution might be expressed like this:

- *P*(one vote for Cesar Chavez Center) = .6
- *P*(no votes for Cesar Chavez Chavez) = .4

To anticipate later, more complex, examples, ask, How might you illustrate this result with a bar graph? In this case, there are only two bars, and the graph might look like this. (This graph is also included on a blackline master.)

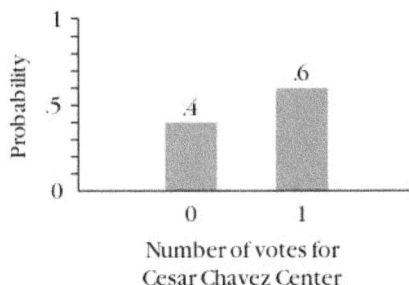

Tell students that a graph like this is called a *probability bar graph.* It is similar to a frequency bar graph, but shows probabilities rather than numbers of occurrences. (The term *histogram* is sometimes used for graphs like this, but some texts use that term in other ways.)

The height of each bar indicates the probability of that result, so the sum of the heights of the bars is 1.

Students will likely see at this stage that there is a similar set of precise probabilities for other sample sizes as well, but that probabilities for larger polls are harder to compute than for the poll of size 1. Acknowledge that they may not yet know what these probabilities are or how to find them, and tell them they will learn this soon.

Key Questions

How might you find these theoretical probabilities?
What might the result be for a 1-person poll?
What is the probability of each possible result?
How might you illustrate this result with a bar graph?

Supplemental Activity

The Tack or the Coin? (reinforcement) has students use results from an experiment to predict what will happen in a future experiment.

"Pennant Fever" Reflection

Intent

Students review the use of combinatorial coefficients for finding probabilities.

Mathematics

The analysis students did in the Year 3 unit *Pennant Fever* is similar to the analysis they will do in *The Theory of Three-Person Polls*. In preparation for that work, this activity reviews ideas from *Pennant Fever*, including the use of combinatorial coefficients in computing probabilities.

Progression

Students revisit and analyze the probabilities from *Pennant Fever* and consider how that situation is similar to or different from the situation in *Sampling Seniors*. The subsequent discussion centers on the use of combinatorial coefficients when calculating probabilities.

Approximate Time

5 to 10 minutes for introduction
30 minutes for activity (at home or in class)
15 to 20 minutes for discussion

Classroom Organization

Individuals or small groups, followed by whole-class discussion

Doing the Activity

You may want to review briefly the baseball-team scenario from *Pennant Fever*.

Discussing and Debriefing the Activity

Give students a few minutes to share their results in their groups before beginning the discussion.

Question 1

For Question 1, you need only establish a general similarity between pulling a sequence of objects from a bag and having the Good Guys play a sequence of games in which they win or lose with a fixed probability. Students might suggest viewing a vote for Cesar Chavez Center as a "win," as that is the majority preference.

Students might observe that the *Pennant Fever* scenario actually involves sampling with replacement while the polling method of *Sampling Seniors* is sampling without replacement. It's fine if they make this distinction without using the formal terminology.

Question 2

For Question 2, get the answer both as $.62^7$ and as a decimal approximation (roughly .0352). Some students might use trees (or partial trees) to explain the process of multiplying probabilities for a sequence of events; others might prefer an area model.

Question 3

By analogy with Question 2, students should see that the probability of a particular sequence of six wins and a loss is $.62^6 \cdot .38$. If necessary, focus on the case of six wins followed by a loss.

The primary purpose of Question 3 is to review, for a simple case, that the probability of the Good Guys winning a particular number of games is not simply a power of .62 times a power of .38. Specifically, there are seven ways the Good Guys can win exactly six games:

- They can win the first six games and lose the last one.
- They can win the first five games, lose the sixth, and win the last one.
- They can win the first four games, lose the fifth, and win the remaining two. And so on.

Each of these sequences has a probability of $.62^6 \cdot .38$, or approximately .0216. Although this is less than the probability of the Good Guys winning all seven games (.0352), the total probability of the Good Guys winning exactly six games is $7 \cdot .62^6 \cdot .38$ (about .151), which is much greater than the probability of them winning all seven games.

If necessary, have students list all the sequences of wins and losses that will result in exactly six wins. Such a list might look like this:

W	W	W	W	W	W	L
W	W	W	W	W	L	W
W	W	W	W	L	W	W
W	W	W	L	W	W	W
W	W	L	W	W	W	W
W	L	W	W	W	W	W
L	W	W	W	W	W	W

Ask, **Can you see that there are seven possibilities without making a list?** The explanation is fairly simple, because there are seven choices for the game the Good Guys lose.

Question 4

For Question 4, students should see that any particular sequence of four wins and three losses has probability $.62^4 \cdot .38^3$, but the counting issue here is more complex than in Question 3. Through a list of cases, students can determine that there are 35 possible sequences. It's helpful to use this discussion to briefly review the concepts of *permutations* and *combinations*.

You might begin by asking, **Do you use permutations or combinations to count the number of ways the Good Guys can win exactly four of their seven games?** Bring out that this is a case for combinations, and review this notation for the number of ways of choosing four objects from a set of seven:

$$_7C_4 \left[\text{or} \begin{pmatrix} 7 \\ 4 \end{pmatrix} \right]$$

There's no need to go into the theory of how to compute $_7C_4$ at this time. Students might get the value 35 using a calculator's $_nC_r$ key from a list of cases, or they may recall how to find it using factorials. They will reexamine the theory in Part II of *Bags of Marbles and Bowls of Ice Cream*.

Be sure students can put the value of $_7C_4$ together with the probability $.62^4 \cdot .38^3$ for each particular sequence to see that the probability of the Good Guys winning exactly four games and losing three is $_7C_4 \cdot .62^4 \cdot 38^3$, or approximately .284.

Key Questions

Can you see that there are seven possibilities without making a list?

Do you use permutations or combinations to count the number of ways the Good Guys can win exactly four of their seven games?

Bags of Marbles and Bowls of Ice Cream

Intent

Students distinguish between sampling with replacement and sampling without replacement.

Mathematics

In Part I, students investigate two approaches to sampling: with and without replacement. In Part II, they use the "cones and bowls" analogy to review the relationship between combinations and permutations.

Progression

In Part I, students discover that when the sample size is much smaller than the population, it doesn't much matter whether sampling is done with or without replacement. In Part II, they continue to review the relationship between permutations and combinations. The subsequent discussion establishes that if the sample size is much smaller than the overall population, sampling with replacement is approximately the same as sampling without replacement.

Approximate Time

30 minutes for activity (at home or in class)
10 to 15 minutes for discussion

Classroom Organization

Individuals or small groups, followed by whole-class discussion

Doing the Activity

This activity requires no introduction.

Discussing and Debriefing the Activity

Part I: With and Without Replacement

Have a couple of students share their findings. It should be obvious that the difference in answers between Questions 2a and 2b is far less than the difference between Questions 1a and 1b.

For Question 1a, the probability is $\frac{2}{4}$, or .5, while for Question 1b, it is $\frac{10}{12}$, or

approximately .8333. For Question 2a, the probability is $\frac{9992}{11992}$, which is

approximately .8332, while for Question 2b, it is approximately .8333.

Ask students, Which type of sampling is easier to analyze? They should see that sampling with replacement is easier, because the probability remains the same for each marble selected.

Help students to see that there is not much numeric difference between the two approaches if the overall population is "big enough." Tell students that for the sake of simplicity, they will assume for the rest of the unit that the overall population is big enough that they can treat the polling problem as if it were with replacement. Add this to your poster of assumptions:

The overall population is big enough compared to the sample size that we can approximate the polling process by using sampling with replacement.

You may want to point out that in practice, this assumption is used in this way:

For each voter picked in the poll, the probability that this voter is in favor of the candidate is equal to the proportion in favor of the candidate in the overall population.

You may also want to mention that in this statistics context, the word *proportion* is used to mean a *fraction,* although in other mathematics settings, a proportion is sometimes an equation stating that two ratios are equal. Throughout this unit, the terms *proportion* and *fraction* are used synonymously.

Ask, What do you call a sequence of events in which the outcome of one event does not affect the outcome of another? Review the phrase **independent events** to describe this. In other words, students can think of sampling with replacement as a sequence of independent events.

A Rule of Thumb

Tell students that one common rule of thumb for when an overall population is big enough to justify the assumption just discussed is that the sample size must be less than 5% of the population size.

Ask, Does this rule of thumb apply to the poll in the central unit problem? In that problem, the polling size is 500, while 5% of 400,000 is 20,000, so sampling with replacement is a reasonable approximation. Emphasize that this is a reasonable assumption to make about all election polls and that the work throughout the rest of the unit is dependent on this assumption.

Part II: Cones and Bowls

Have a volunteer explain his or her work on Question 4. He or she likely will point out that Johanna has 20 choices for her first flavor, 19 remaining choices for her second flavor, and 18 remaining choices for her third flavor, which yields $20 \cdot 19 \cdot 18 = 6840$ choices.

Ask students why the values 20, 19, and 18 are multiplied here, not added. Get a clear explanation, perhaps with a tree diagram.

For Question 5, the presenter might build on the work with Question 4, essentially answering Question 6 at the same time. The key idea is that any *set* of three flavors leads to six different cones but only one bowl, so there are six times as many cones as bowls. Put another way, there are one-sixth as many bowls as cones, so Jonathan has $6840 \div 6 = 1140$ options.

You may want to have students use their calculators to verify that $_{20}C_3 = 1140$.

As needed, go over Question 7, focusing on the specific number that relates Jonathan's bowls to Johanna's cones. Students should recognize that there are 24 cones for each bowl. Help them to see that the number 24 here is 4!. Also bring out that in general, the number of r-scoop cones and the number of r-scoop bowls have this relationship:

$$\text{number of bowls} = \frac{\text{number of cones}}{r!}$$

Key Questions

What do you call a sequence of events in which the outcome of one event does not affect the outcome of another?
Does this rule of thumb apply to the poll in the central unit problem?
Why do you multiply the values 20, 19, and 18?

Polls and Pennant Fever

Intent

In these activities, students begin to explore the effect of sample size on the probability that a poll will correctly predict a particular result.

Mathematics

By constructing and comparing probability distributions of sample proportions for polls with progressively larger sample sizes, students observe several key ideas. They notice that the larger the poll size, (1) the more the distribution of sample proportions is concentrated around the true proportion, (2) the more likely it is that the poll will correctly identify the candidate who is actually leading, and (3) the more the probability distribution of sample proportions looks like a normal distribution. This last finding is expressed as the **central limit theorem.**

Progression

In *The Theory of Three-Person Polls*, students find the probability distribution for a 3-person poll of a given population. They look at the effect on the probability distribution if the true proportion is larger or smaller in *Graphs of the Theory*. They then investigate the effect of increasing sample size in *The Theory of Polls* and *Civics in Action*, leading to the introduction of the central limit theorem.

The Theory of Three-Person Polls
Graphs of the Theory
The Theory of Polls
Civics in Action

The Theory of 3-Person Polls

Intent

Students find the probability distribution of sampling results for a 3-person poll.

Mathematics

Students apply their knowledge of probability distributions to the case of a 3-person poll. They observe that this is an example of a binomial distribution. The discussion points out that, in an election, it is not the *number* of votes that is of interest, but the *proportion* of votes. The proportion actually supporting a candidate in an election poll is known as the **true proportion,** while the fraction of the polling sample in favor of the candidate is the **sample proportion.**

Progression

Students list the possible outcomes for a 3-person poll, find the probability for each possible outcome, and make a probability bar graph showing the results. The subsequent discussion reviews the term *binomial distribution* for situations like sampling with replacement. It is suggested that it is more useful to express the polling results in terms of proportions than numbers of votes, and the probability distribution graph is revised to reflect proportions. The discussion also introduces the terms *true proportion* and *sample proportion*, and the associated notation, p and $\hat{p}$, respectively.

Approximate Time

35 minutes

Classroom Organization

Individuals or small groups, followed by whole-class discussion

Materials

Optional: Transparency of *The Theory of Three-Person Polls* blackline master

Doing the Activity

In this activity, students consider polls of size 3 and find the theoretical probability of each possible result (0 "yes" votes, 1 "yes" vote, 2 "yes" votes, or 3 "yes" votes). Tell them to make use of the assumption discussed in *Bags of Marbles and*

Bowls of Ice Cream by using sampling *with* replacement, even though the polling situation inherently involves sampling *without* replacement.

For Question 2, if needed, suggest groups think of the votes as being pulled out of a bag one at a time and consider what sequences of results could occur. They should see each 3-person poll is a sequence of "yes" and "no" votes, such as YYN and NYN.

Discussing and Debriefing the Activity

Have two or three groups present their results and explanations. For simplicity, have students identify outcomes by the number of "yes" votes. They should see that the possible outcomes and their probabilities are as follows:

- $P(0$ "yes" votes$) = .4^3 = .064$
- $P(1$ "yes" vote$) = 3 \cdot .4^2 \cdot .6 = .288$
- $P(2$ "yes" votes$) = 3 \cdot .4 \cdot .6^2 = .432$
- $P(3$ "yes" votes$) = .6^3 = .216$

Ask, for the case of one or two "yes" votes, Where does the coefficient 3 come from? For example, students should see that the probability of exactly one "yes" vote is $3 \cdot .4^2 \cdot .6$. This is because a single sequence, such as NNY, has probability $.4^2 \cdot .6$, and there are three "1-yes" sequences (NNY, NYN, and YNN).

The Binomial Distribution

Ask students, Where have you seen probabilities found in this way before? The probabilities here are found exactly like those in *Pennant Fever*, which students reviewed in *"Pennant Fever" Reflection*.

For instance, in Question 4 of that activity, they found that the probability of the Good Guys getting exactly four wins out of seven games is $_7C_4 \cdot .62^4 \cdot 38^3$. Help students see that the coefficient 3, for the 1-"yes" polling result, can be thought of as $_3C_1$.

Ask, What is the general term for a set of probabilities involving repeated, identical independent events with two outcomes? If needed, remind the class of the term **binomial distribution.** Bring out that this distribution depends on two parameters, usually labeled n and p.

What do the parameters n and p represent in a *Pennant Fever* problem or a polling situation? Students should see that n represents either the number of games played or the number of people in a poll, while p represents the probability of winning each game or the proportion of "yes" voters in the overall population. Why do we use the letter p to represent both the true proportion in a population and the probability of success in a binomial trial? Students should be able to explain that in a poll, the theoretical probability of success for a single person polled (that is, of a "yes" vote) is precisely the proportion of the population that supports the candidate.

Review that in general, each repetition of the event is called a *trial,* and we designate one of the two outcomes as a *success.* Therefore, *n* represents the number of trials, and *p* represents the probability of success.

Transition to Proportions

Point out that in an election, what matters is not the *number* of votes, but the *proportion* of votes. Coretta doesn't really care how many votes she gets as long as it's a majority.

Review the term **true proportion** (used in the activity) to represent the proportion supporting a given candidate in the overall population, and tell students that this value is often represented by the letter *p*. Basically, the purpose of taking a poll is to find out what the true proportion is—that is, to find the numeric value of *p*. You might mention that the true proportion is often given as a percentage, but it can also be given as a fraction or decimal.

When we take a poll, we get a certain number of voters for the candidate and a certain number against. From these, we can compute the fraction in favor of the candidate, which is called the **sample proportion**. This sample proportion is often our best estimate for the true proportion.

To clarify the concept, ask, What could the sample proportion be in a 3-person poll? Students should see that it could be 0%, $33\frac{1}{3}$%, $66\frac{2}{3}$%, or 100%.

Tell students that the usual symbol for the sample proportion is $\hat{p}$, which is read as "p hat." In other words, when we take a poll, $\hat{p}$ represents the proportion (that is, the fraction) of people supporting the candidate *among those polled*.

Question 3

Have a volunteer share the probability bar graph for the group's results, showing each of the possible outcomes. It should look something like this:

Distribution of 3-person polls with true proportion = 60%

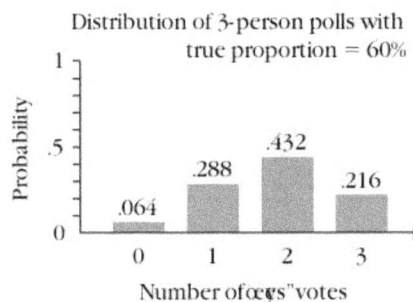

Tell students that it's often more useful to express the outcome using the sample proportion of "yes" votes rather than the number of "yes" votes. Then ask, How would you change the graph to show the sample proportion rather than the number of "yes" votes? They should see that they need only to change the labeling of the horizontal axis, and they should come up with a graph like the next one. (This graph is also included on a blackline master.)

Distribution of 3-person polls with true proportion = 60%

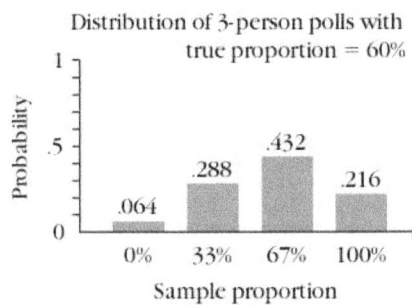

Ask students what the graph says. For instance, they should be able to articulate that the height .432 for the 67% bar means that if one conducts a random poll of size 3 from this population, the probability of getting exactly two "yes" votes (and one "no" vote) is .432. Be sure students see that the probability .432 depends on the true proportion, which in this activity is .6.

Comparison with "Sampling Seniors" Results

Ask students, How do your results from *Sampling Seniors* compare to the probability distribution you just developed?

Although those results probably won't match the theory perfectly, they should confirm the general pattern of the theoretical analysis, with the 2-yes outcome the most likely, the 1-yes and 3-yes outcomes roughly equally likely, and the 0-yes outcome least likely. Help students see that if they continued doing 3-person polls, the frequency of occurrence for each possible result would match the theoretical probabilities more and more closely.

Does the Poll Predict Correctly?

Point out that the main issue in an election is "Who wins?" and that the true proportion in today's activity was 60%. Ask, Which outcomes show a "correct" poll?

Students should see that both the 2-yes and 3-yes outcomes represent "correct" polls, with a combined probability of about 65% (.432 + .216). Thus, a 3-person poll is not very reliable. Even in this case, where the overall population is solidly in favor (60% "yes" versus 40% "no"), more than a third of all 3-person polls will fail to predict the outcome correctly.

You might have students compare this aspect of the theoretical distribution to the corresponding results from *Sampling Seniors*.

If you have additional time, you can have students go through a similar analysis as in *The Theory of Three-Person Polls* but using a different value for the true proportion. *Graphs of the Theory* also continues this idea.

Key Questions

Where does the coefficient 3 come from?
Where have you seen probabilities found in this way before?
What is the general term for a set of probabilities involving repeated, identical independent events with two outcomes?
What do the parameters n and p represent in a *Pennant Fever* problem or a polling situation?
Why do we use the letter p to represent both the true proportion in a population and the probability of success in a binomial trial?
What could the sample proportion be in a 3-person poll?
How would you change the graph to show the sample proportion rather than the number of "yes" votes?
How do your results from *Sampling Seniors* compare to the probability distribution you just developed?
Which outcomes show a "correct" poll?

Graphs of the Theory

Intent

Students investigate the effect of changing the overall population (the true proportion) on the theoretical distribution of poll results.

Mathematics

This activity continues the theme of *The Theory of Three-Person Polls*, with students making graphs using other true proportions. Students observe that as the true proportion increases, the probability bar graph shifts to the right. They also develop expressions for the probability of each outcome in terms of the true proportion.

Progression

Graphs of the Theory is essentially a continuation of *The Theory of Three-Person Polls*. Students now construct probability distributions for 3-person polls in two more populations, which have different true proportions. They are then asked to generalize their work for a true proportion of *p* and to speculate on the effect of increasing the sample size.

Approximate Time

30 minutes for activity (at home or in class)
10 minutes for discussion

Classroom Organization

Individuals, followed by whole-class discussion

Materials

Optional: Transparencies of *Graphs of the Theory* blackline masters

Doing the Activity

This activity requires no introduction.

Discussing and Debriefing the Activity

Have groups discuss Question 3 while one group prepares to present its graphs for Question 1 and another group does so for Question 2.

Questions 1 and 2

Questions 1 and 2 are primarily for review and to bring out the idea that the probabilities change when the true proportion changes.

Probability bar graphs for the two situations look like this. (Both graphs are available as blackline masters. Note that because of rounding, the probabilities for the first graph do not total exactly 1.)

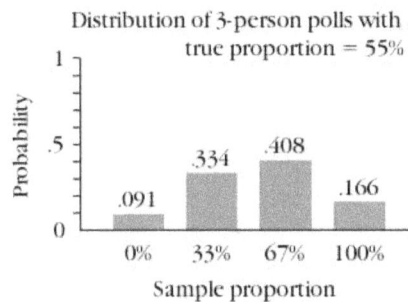

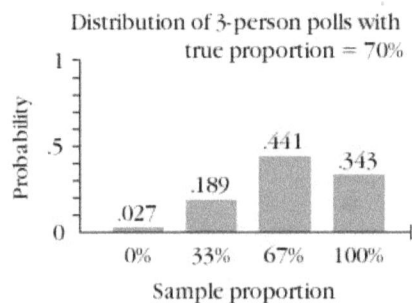

Distribution of 3-person polls with true proportion = 55%

Probability (y-axis, from 0 to 1)
Sample proportion (x-axis: 0%, 33%, 67%, 100%)

- 0%: .091
- 33%: .334
- 67%: .408
- 100%: .166

Distribution of 3-person polls with true proportion = 70%

Probability (y-axis, from 0 to 1)
Sample proportion (x-axis: 0%, 33%, 67%, 100%)

- 0%: .027
- 33%: .189
- 67%: .441
- 100%: .343

Students may describe the differences between the graphs in various ways, such as these:

- "The graph for 70% has been shifted to the right, compared to the graph for 55%."
- "With a true proportion of 70%, you will be more likely to get two or three 'yes' votes and less likely to get one or zero 'yes' votes as compared to the graph for 55%."

Have students compare these graphs with the case of a true proportion of 60% (from *The Theory of Three-Person Polls* and available as a blackline master).

Emphasize that each graph represents a case of the binomial distribution for $n = 3$ and a particular value of p.

Question 3

Students should generalize Questions 1 and 2 to find the probability distribution for a 3-person poll with true proportion p. If needed, ask specifically what the probability of a "no" vote is for a particular voter, and help students see that it is $1 - p$. Students should get these results:

- $P(0$ "yes" votes$) = (1 - p)^3$
- $P(1$ "yes" vote$) = 3p(1 - p)^2$
- $P(2$ "yes" votes$) = 3p^2(1 - p)$
- $P(3$ "yes" votes$) = p^3$

Explain that these probabilities represent the general version of the case $n = 3$ of the binomial distribution. You might point out that these expressions have coefficients 1, 3, 3, and 1 (although the 1s are implicit) and that these numbers are binomial (or combinatorial) coefficients. You might also mention that they form a row of Pascal's triangle.

Question 4

The main focus of the discussion should be on Question 4, which leads into *The Theory of Polls*. Let students share ideas on the effect of changing the sample size.

In *The Theory of Polls*, students will see that for larger polls, the graph will be "bunched" closer around the true proportion. Focus their attention in this direction with such general questions as, How "spread out" would the bars be? Where would they cluster? Students may intuitively sense that a larger poll is more likely to give a result close to the true proportion. (They'll see more about the effect of increasing sample size in the next activity.)

Students may make other observations about the effect of increasing sample size on the graph. For example, they may point out that there will be more bars and that each individual probability will be smaller (because there are more possible sample proportions). Do not neglect these ideas, but be sure to at least raise the issue of the spread of the data.

Key Questions

How "spread out" would the bars be? Where would they cluster?

The Theory of Polls

Intent

This activity prepares students for the introduction of the central limit theorem.

Mathematics

Students use combinatorial coefficients to find the theoretical distribution of poll results for polls of various sizes. The discussion of the activity will strengthen their understanding of how to find these probabilities and lead to the observation that as sample size increases, the probability bar graph begins to look more like the normal distribution. The central limit theorem expresses this fact.

Progression

Students find theoretical probability distributions for polls of several sizes. In the follow-up discussion, the class reviews the use of combinatorial coefficients to get the probabilities and discusses the probability of a "correct" poll prediction. The class then compares the probability bar graphs for $n = 5$ and $n = 9$ and notes that the graph is beginning to resemble the normal curve. The graph for the case $n = 50$ is used to emphasize the resemblance to the normal curve and to state the central limit theorem for this context.

Approximate Time

40 minutes

Classroom Organization

Small groups, followed by whole-class discussion

Materials

Optional: Transparencies of *The Theory of Polls* blackline masters

Doing the Activity

Tell students they will now focus on what happens as the poll size increases. Point out that for the sake of making clear comparisons among different sample sizes, the true proportion is fixed at 60%.

Talk about the fact that we are interested in the theoretical distribution of poll results in order to understand the reliability of polls. While an individual poll has many possible outcomes, some results are much more likely than others. We want to know the likelihood of getting a sample proportion "close to" the true proportion.

One question of particular interest is the likelihood of correctly predicting the winner of the election. As students saw in *The Theory of Three-Person Polls*, if the candidate has the support of 60% of the overall population, there is about a 65% chance that a 3-person poll will show that candidate leading.

Let students begin work on the activity in groups. As you observe, you may decide it's worthwhile to bring the class together to go over a single case, such as the probability of getting two "yes" votes and three "no" votes (that is, a sample proportion of 40%) in Question 1a. Use the ideas below as a guideline for this case.

You also may want to bring the class together when most groups are done with the case of 5-person polls, discuss this case, and review the use of combinatorial coefficients. Groups can then work on the case of 9-person polls.

Discussing and Debriefing the Activity

Question 1: The 5-Person Poll

Have several students explain how to get each probability for Question 1a. For example, to find the probability of getting two "yes" votes and three "no" votes, they may begin with the fact that the probability of any *particular* sequence of two "yes" votes and three "no" votes (such as YNNYN) is $.6^2 \cdot .4^3$. To clarify this, you may want to suggest they view a sample of size 5 as a *sequence* of five individuals, like the sequence of games in a *Pennant Fever* problem (see "*Pennant Fever*" *Reflection*), rather than as a set of five people chosen all at once.

The presenter might then explain that there are ten such sequences (perhaps by making a list of cases), so the probability of getting two "yes" votes and three "no" votes is given by the expression $10 \cdot .6^2 \cdot .4^3$, which is .2304.

Ask students to explain what this number represents. They should be able to articulate that if the true proportion for the population is 60%, then about 23% of all 5-person polls will result in two "yes" votes and three "no" votes.

Using Combinatorial Coefficients

Before moving on to study the probabilities more closely, review the use of combinatorial coefficients for expressing these values.

Ask, **What symbol can we use to express the number of sequences with two "yes" votes and three "no" votes?** Review that the number 10, in the expression $10 \cdot .6^2 \cdot .4^3$, is the combinatorial coefficient $_5C_2$. If needed, review the connection between the counting process here and that in the *Pennant Fever* scenario.

How can you find numeric values for combinatorial coefficients on your calculator? As needed, go over the mechanics of this process. (It is not necessary for students to know the formula for computing these combinatorial coefficients in this unit. Use your judgment about whether to review this.)

The Probability Bar Graph

After all the probabilities have been found, have a group display its probability bar graph for the 5-person poll, or use a transparency of the graph shown here. (The possible poll results—that is, the sample proportions given on the horizontal axis—are shown here as percentages, but they could also be shown as fractions or decimals.)

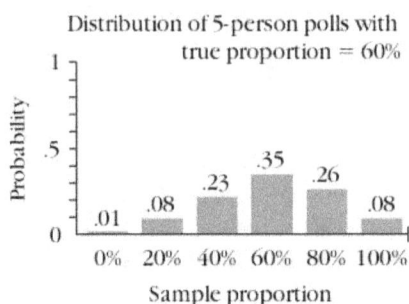

You may want to compare this graph to that for the case of 3-person polls, or you may prefer to wait until after discussing Question 2 (the case of 9-person polls).

In the case of 5-person polls, as in Question 1c, there is about a 68% chance. (If students use the rounded values shown in the graph, they will find the sum .08 + .26 + .35, which is .69, but the actual probability is closer to .68.)

Students should see that the chance of a "correct' poll is still fairly low but that it is up slightly from the figure of 65% for 3-person polls.

Question 2: The 9-Person Poll

If students had trouble getting the probabilities for the 5-person poll, you may want to give groups more time to work on the 9-person poll before proceeding with the discussion.

Let other students give probabilities for different possible results for a 9-person poll, expressing the results using combinatorial coefficients.

At this stage, students should be fairly comfortable with the idea that in an *n*-person poll from a population with a true proportion *p*, the probability of getting exactly *r* "yes" votes is $_nC_r \cdot p^r \cdot (1 - p)^{n-r}$.

Then have a group display its probability bar graph for the 9-person poll, or use a transparency of the graph shown here. Notice that this graph has a different vertical scale from the graphs for *n* = 3 and *n* = 5. Because there are more possible results, each result has a smaller probability than in the earlier cases. (You may want to emphasize that the probabilities for sample proportions of 0% and 11% are not actually 0, but that the probabilities shown in the graph are rounded to the nearest hundredth. This rounding is also the reason that the sum of the probabilities is not exactly 1 for either the 5-person or the 9-person graph.)

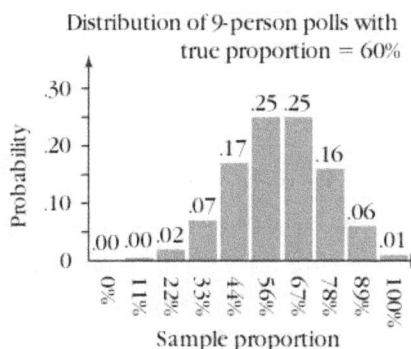

Distribution of 9-person polls with true proportion = 60%

Before comparing graphs, ask, **What is the likelihood of a correct prediction?** Students should see that this has now risen to about 73% and that the chance for error is diminishing as the poll size grows.

Comparing the Graphs

Ask, **What is happening to the graph of the theoretical distribution as the sample size gets larger?** To bring out the changes, you can use a set of graphs with a common scale and bars of a fixed width. Try to elicit this conclusion, and post this principle:

> **The larger the poll size, the more the theoretical distribution of sample proportions is concentrated around the true proportion.**

If students don't see a clear pattern, show them the graph for the 50-person case. If possible, however, hold off showing this graph until the discussion of the normal curve in the next section ("The Normal Distribution and the Central Limit Theorem"). If anyone suggests the results are getting closer to a normal distribution, you can jump ahead to that material, but be sure to come back to the ideas in the next few paragraphs.

What happens to the percentage of "correct" polls (that is, those that show the true leader actually ahead) as the poll size increases? Review the values found so far:

- For 3-person polls: Approximately 65% of polls are "correct."
- For 5-person polls: Approximately 68% of polls are "correct."
- For 9-person polls: Approximately 73% of polls are "correct."

This should lead students to this very reasonable principle:

The larger the poll size, the more likely it is for the person who is actually leading in the race to be the winner in the poll.

You might also ask, in light of this principle, Why wouldn't a pollster simply use a large poll size to get a high probability of picking the winner correctly? A larger poll requires greater resources, and pollsters need to balance cost with the desire for accurate results.

The Normal Distribution and the Central Limit Theorem

Have students look at the probability bar graph for 9-person polls, and ask, Does this graph suggest anything to you? Does its shape look familiar? Have them imagine what would happen as the poll size continued to grow. You may want to sketch a curve along the outline of the tops of the bars to suggest what happens as poll size increases.

If no one mentions the normal distribution, show students the graph below for the case of a 50-person poll. (This graph is also included on a blackline master.) Point out that probabilities for sample proportions below 40% or above 80% are not zero, but are so small they don't show up.

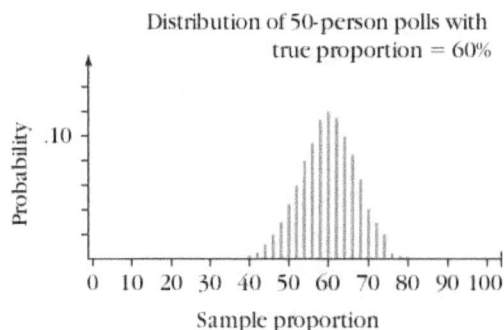

Distribution of 50-person polls with true proportion = 60%

Students may not remember many details about the normal distribution, but they should remember the general shape of the curve. If this graph does not elicit recollection of the normal distribution, mention the term yourself. (Students can see examples of normal curves in *The Central Limit Theorem*.)

Explain that the connection between polls and the normal distribution is part of a profound principle in mathematics called the **central limit theorem.** (This unit treats only a special case of this theorem. *The Central Limit Theorem: An Overview for Teachers* contains a more general statement of the theorem for your reference.)

Before stating the theorem, ask students to review the situation. Help them to articulate that we are considering a population with a given overall proportion p in favor of the candidate. We take a poll of size n and find the proportion in favor of the candidate among the people polled. You may want to review the terms *true proportion* and *sample proportion* and remind students that we generally represent these by the symbols p and $\hat{p}$, respectively.

Students have seen that for any given value of n, they can find the theoretical probability of obtaining each possible sample proportion. Therefore, for a given poll of size n and true proportion p, there is a probability distribution of sample proportions.

Then, post this statement of the central limit theorem:

> **As the poll size gets larger, the probability distribution of sample proportions looks more and more like a normal distribution.**

Remind students that there are many normal distributions. Also point out that the normal distribution that approximates a given poll depends on the true proportion for the overall population and on the poll size. Review the earlier observation that as the poll size increases, the distribution becomes more concentrated around the true proportion.

Tell students there is no easy rule of thumb about how big a poll should be to have the theoretical distribution look "close enough" to normal. This depends on the true proportion for the overall population (and on what "close enough" means).

For the rest of the unit, we will assume that the sample sizes given in problems and those selected in student projects are large enough that the normal distribution is a good approximation. You can add this to the list of assumptions posted during the discussion of *The Pollster's Dilemma*.

How Does the Central Limit Theorem Fit Into the Unit?

Ask students, How do you think you might use the central limit theorem in the unit? Let them share ideas, which will probably be fairly speculative at this point. Then tell them they will be learning more this theorem and about the normal distribution and will see how these ideas can be used to understand the unit problem.

Also explain that the central limit theorem applies to many other situations involving averaging. You might briefly indicate how the sample proportion for a poll is a kind of average. Emphasize that this theorem helps to explain why the normal distribution is so important in the study of statistics. The theorem shows that normal distributions pop up of their own accord every time we do averaging.

Key Questions

What symbol can we use to express the number of sequences with two "yes" votes and three "no" votes?

How can you find numeric values for combinatorial coefficients on your calculator?

What is the likelihood of a correct prediction?

What is happening to the graph of the theoretical distribution as the sample size gets larger?

What happens to the percentage of "correct" polls (that is, those that show the true leader actually ahead) as the poll size increases?

Why wouldn't a pollster simply use a large poll size to get a high probability of picking the winner correctly?

Does the graph for 9-person polls suggest anything to you? Does its shape look familiar?

How do you think you might use the central limit theorem in the unit?

The Central Limit Theorem: An Overview for Teachers

This unit treats only a special case of the central limit theorem: its application to the binomial distribution. In this unit, the binomial distribution occurs as a result of a process of sampling with replacement from a population with two groups (those favoring the candidate and those opposing the candidate). In the Year 3 unit *Pennant Fever,* the binomial distribution arises through repeated trials of the same two-outcome event.

Sampling with replacement and repeated trials of an event are essentially two different settings for the same mathematical situation. This discussion of the more general statement of the central limit theorem uses the sampling situation, as sampling is the context of *The Pollster's Dilemma*.

Imagine a bin containing many small, numbered balls. Such a bin represents a discrete probability distribution, with each number having a specific probability. (For the central problem of this unit, you can imagine a bin containing only 0s and 1s, with 1s representing votes for the candidate and 0s representing votes for the opponent.)

Now imagine taking a large sample (with replacement) from the bin and then finding the average—the mean—of the results. In other words, simply add the numbers on the sampled balls and divide by the number of balls chosen. (If you do this for the bin of 0s and 1s, the average is the *sample proportion*. For instance, if you pick fifty-eight 1s and forty-two 0s, the sum is 58 and the average is 0.58, which corresponds to a sample proportion of 58%.)

As with the results in *The Theory of Polls,* the possible average for a sample of a given size will have some probability distribution. That is, each possible outcome for the average will have a precise probability, which depends on the size of the sample and on the distribution of values within the bin. (The probability bar graphs for *The Theory of Three-Person Polls*, *Graphs of the Theory*, and *The Theory of Polls*, which give the distribution for the sample proportion for polls of various sizes, are examples of the distribution of such an average.)

It's natural to expect the distribution of these averages to center around the mean for the entire bin (just as you expect sample proportions to center around the true proportion). And the larger the sample, the closer you would expect the average to be to the mean for the bin. The central limit theorem states both of these things, and more.

Specifically, suppose μ is the mean and σ is the standard deviation for the bin. That is, consider the number on each ball as a separate data item, and let μ and σ be the mean and standard deviation of this data set. Let X represent the average for a sample (with replacement) of n items from the bin. We are interested in the probability distribution for X.

The central limit theorem states, in effect:

If n is "large enough," the probability distribution for X is approximately a normal distribution with mean μ and standard deviation $\dfrac{\sigma}{\sqrt{n}}$.

Notice in particular that as n increases, the standard deviation for X decreases.

More precisely, the theorem states that as n gets large, the distribution of the expression $\dfrac{X - \mu}{(\sigma / \sqrt{n})}$ approaches the standard normal distribution, which is the normal distribution with mean 0 and standard deviation 1.

The central limit theorem can even be generalized to the situation in which each item in the sample is drawn from a different bin. In that case, the value μ is replaced by the average of the means of the individual bins, and the value $\dfrac{\sigma}{\sqrt{n}}$ is replaced by the expression

$$\frac{1}{n}\sqrt{\sum_{i=1}^{n} \sigma_i^2}$$

where the values σ_i are the standard deviations for the individual bins. If the values σ_i are all equal to the same value σ, this expression simplifies to $\dfrac{\sigma}{\sqrt{n}}$.

An Example

To see a very simple example of what is meant by "the probability distribution for X," consider a bin containing forty 1s, forty 2s, fifteen 3s, and five 10s. For this bin, you can compute that the mean is 2.15 and the standard deviation is approximately 1.93. (A spinner representing the same probability distribution is the subject of *A Plus for the Community*.)

If two balls are drawn (with replacement) from this bin, the possible results, with their probabilities, are as follows:

- $P(\text{two 1s}) = .4^2$
- $P(\text{one 1, one 2}) = 2 \cdot .4^2$
- $P(\text{one 1, one 3}) = 2 \cdot .4 \cdot .15$
- $P(\text{one 1, one 10}) = 2 \cdot .4 \cdot .05$
- $P(\text{two 2s}) = .4^2$
- $P(\text{one 2, one 3}) = 2 \cdot .4 \cdot .15$
- $P(\text{one 2, one 10}) = 2 \cdot .4 \cdot .05$
- $P(\text{two 3s}) = .15^2$
- $P(\text{one 3, one 10}) = 2 \cdot .15 \cdot .05$
- $P(\text{two 10s}) = .05^2$

Each possible outcome of two balls has an average. For instance, if you draw a 1 and a 2, the average is 1.5. This outcome has probability $2 \cdot .4^2$, so $P(X = 1.5) = 2 \cdot .4^2 = .32$. Notice that an average of 2 can be obtained either by drawing a 1 and a 3 or by drawing two 2s, so $P(X = 2) = (2 \cdot .4 \cdot .15) + (.4^2) = .28$. Similarly, every other possible value for X has a specific probability. This analysis leads to the probability distribution for X for a sample of size 2.

The same sort of analysis can be done for samples of size 3, size 4, and so on, and each analysis gives the probability distribution for X for samples of that size. The central limit theorem states that if n is big, the distribution of X for a sample of size n is approximately a normal distribution with mean 2.15 and standard deviation $\frac{1.93}{\sqrt{n}}$.

The supplemental activity *Another View of the Central Limit Theorem* gives students an opportunity to examine a similar situation in more detail and see for themselves what happens to the distribution of these averages.

Civics in Action

Intent

This activity involves another look at the probabilities for correctly predicting the winner of an election using a small poll.

Mathematics

This activity once more highlights the idea that a larger sample size will generally lead to more certainty about an election outcome.

Progression

Students find the probability that a poll will correctly predict the winner of a particular election for sample sizes of one person, three people, and a larger number of the students' choice. They also speculate about the smallest sample they would be satisfied with. The follow-up discussion brings out that a small poll is likely to give the right prediction in this problem, because p is large.

Approximate Time

20 to 25 minutes for activity (at home or in class)
5 to 10 minutes for discussion

Classroom Organization

Individuals, followed by whole-class discussion

Doing the Activity

This activity requires no introduction.

Discussing and Debriefing the Activity

In the discussion following *Bags of Marbles and Bowls of Ice Cream*, students were given a rule of thumb about when they can safely use sampling with replacement in modeling the polling process. According to that rule of thumb, sampling with replacement gives a good approximation whenever the sample size is less than 5% of the overall population. In this activity, the overall population is only 60 students, so any poll of more than 3 students would violate this rule of thumb. Thus, the probabilities students found for larger polls were not very accurate. You may want to bring this out in the course of the discussion.

Ask students to try to come to agreement in their groups about the poll size Clarissa needs. Their ideas may vary widely, so it may be hard for them to reach a consensus.

Ask a student in each group to report the group's decision and reasoning. They will probably cite results from Questions 1 and 2 in support of their position. Review the details of these questions as needed.

Presumably, students saw that Clarissa has a probability of $\frac{5}{6} \approx 83\%$ of getting the right answer from a 1-person poll. Here are the probabilities needed for Question 2:

- $P(3 \text{ votes for Clarence}) = \left(\frac{5}{6}\right)^3 \approx .58$

- $P(2 \text{ votes for Clarence}) = 3 \cdot \left(\frac{5}{6}\right)^2 \cdot \frac{1}{6} \approx .35$

Thus, Clarissa has about a 93% chance of making the right prediction from a 3-person poll. That may be good enough odds for her. (Using a 5-person poll raises the probability to about 96.5%.)

Ask students to recall their results along these lines from *The Theory of Polls*. They saw in that activity that when 60% of the overall population favors one candidate, a 5-person poll will show that person as the winner only about 68% of the time, and even a 9-person poll yields the correct winner only about 73% of the time.

Students should see that Clarissa can get by with a small poll in this case, but only because the true proportion is so high. If she did not know how people were going to vote, she wouldn't know that a small poll would suffice. (And, of course, if she knew how people were going to vote, she wouldn't need to take a poll at all.)

In the real world, most elections are much closer than Clarence's, so much larger polls are needed. Learning how to choose an appropriate poll size is an important component of this unit.

Ask students to imagine a situation in which the election was close and they needed to find out if a 500-person poll would correctly predict the winner. (Of course, the overall population would have to be much larger than the senior class in this activity.) Students should see that if they use the method from the smaller polls considered so far, the number crunching would be quite formidable (although computers would be helpful). Help them see that choosing a poll size requires deciding how sure they want to be of getting the right answer and making some assumption about how close the election will be.

Normal Distributions Revisited

Intent

In these activities, students extend their knowledge of normal distributions.

Mathematics

Within the limitations of the assumptions for the central unit problem, the preceding work has established that poll results follow a binomial distribution and, for large polls, that binomial distributions resemble normal distributions. Students now go on to review and expand upon what they know about normal distributions in preparation for seeing how to apply this knowledge to a poll. They also learn how to use a table of normal probabilities to calculate areas under the normal curve that have boundaries that are not an integer number of standard deviations from the mean.

Progression

The initial review of the basic facts related to normal distributions is accompanied by a formal statement of the central limit theorem in the reference page *The Central Limit Theorem*. Students continue this review with some practice applying the facts of standard deviation in *Deviations of Swinging*, *Means and More in Middletown*, and *Gifts Aren't Always Free*. In *Graphing Distributions*, they observe the effect on a normal curve of changes in the mean and standard deviation.

With this review behind them, students now learn to work with areas under the normal curve that have more arbitrary boundaries than they have seen in the past. They estimate such areas in *Normal Areas*, motivating the need for the table of normal probabilities, introduced in the reference page *The Normal Table*. They learn to use this table in *More Middletown Musings* and *Back to the Circus*. *Gaps in the Table* teaches them how to use linear interpolation in association with the table.

A Normal Poll brings all of this back into the context of the central unit problem, as students apply the central limit theorem to a polling situation. *A Plus for the Community* leads into the next section, *Means and Standard Deviations*.

Reference: The Central Limit Theorem
Deviations of Swinging
Means and More in Middletown
Graphing Distributions
Gifts Aren't Always Free
Normal Areas
Reference: The Normal Table
More Middletown Musings

Back to the Circus
Gaps in the Table
A Normal Poll
A Plus for the Community

Reference: The Central Limit Theorem

Intent

These pages provide reference material on the central limit theorem.

Mathematics

In the discussion of this material, students review the probabilities for intervals of one and two standard deviations about the mean for normal distributions.

Progression

A class discussion introduces this reference material. The class reviews students' experiences with the normal distribution. Students are reminded that, in general, standard deviation measures the "spread" of data, and they review the probabilities associated with intervals of one and two standard deviations about the mean for normal distributions.

Approximate Time

20 to 30 minutes

Classroom Organization

Whole-class discussion

Doing the Activity

Begin by reviewing the results of the discussion of *The Theory of Polls*, especially these two key principles:

> **The larger the poll size, the more the theoretical distribution of sample proportions is concentrated around the true proportion. As the poll size gets larger, the probability distribution of sample proportions looks more and more like a normal distribution.**

Tell students that the key to the unit problem will be combining these two principles. To help them relate these principles to their previous experience, you might use the idea that taking a poll is like taking a physical measurement, such as finding the period of a pendulum.

To connect the first principle to this analogy, explain that the sample proportion in a poll is, in essence, an average of the views of the people polled. A single measurement gives only an *estimate* of the "true" value. Similarly, a small poll (especially a 1-person poll) gives only an *estimate* of the true proportion supporting a given candidate.

The first principle states, in effect, that just as averaging many measurements gives a better estimate than averaging only a few, a large poll generally gives a better estimate than a small one.

The Normal Distribution

Begin the review of the material in the reference pages by having students share ideas about this question: In what context have you used the concept of normal distribution before? Go over the basic facts about the normal distribution, which are summarized in the student reference pages.

Standard Deviation

Then ask, What concept was used to describe the amount of variation among repetitions of a given experiment? Review the term *standard deviation*.

You might have students do focused free-writing on their ideas about standard deviation and then share what they recall. Review the ideas that a large standard deviation means there is a lot of variation from one experiment to the next, while a small standard deviation means repeated experiments give very similar results.

Bring out that for normal distributions, the likelihood of a particular result depends on how many standard deviations it is from the "true" measurement. (*Note:* Students will not need to compute any standard deviations until after *Mean and Standard Deviation for Probability*. The computation steps will be reviewed then, so the discussion here can focus on the general concept.)

Numeric Connections Between Standard Deviation and Normal Distributions

If students do not mention it themselves, ask specifically, How are probabilities for a normal distribution related to standard deviation? If necessary, remind them that when a set of data is normally distributed, approximately 68% of all results are within one standard deviation of the mean and approximately 95% are within two standard deviations of the mean.

The Central Limit Theorem

The reference pages briefly review the special case of the central limit theorem used in this unit and summarize basic facts about the binomial distribution, normal distributions, and standard deviation. These ideas, which should all have been part of your classroom discussions, are included in the student text for reference.

You may want to use this opportunity to reiterate the assumption that the overall population is sufficiently large that sampling with replacement is a good model for the polling process.

Discrete Versus Continuous Distributions

This is also a good opportunity to discuss the difference between a *discrete* distribution, such as the binomial distribution, which gives the probability of getting each particular event, and a *continuous* distribution, such as the normal distribution, which gives the probability of getting a result within any given interval.

Key Questions

In what context have you used the concept of normal distribution before?
What concept was used to describe the amount of variation among repetitions of a given experiment?
How are probabilities for a normal distribution related to standard deviation?

Supplemental Activity

***Three-Person Races* (extension)** has students explore the theoretical probability distribution of sample proportions for the much more difficult situation of a race with an arbitrary number of candidates.

Deviations of Swinging

Intent

Students apply basic numeric facts relating standard deviation to normal distributions.

Mathematics

This activity requires students to make use of the facts that 68% of normally distributed data will lie within one standard deviation of the mean and 95% will lie within two standard deviations of the mean.

Progression

Given the mean and standard deviation of a set of experimental data, students determine what percentage of future measurements should lie within each of several ranges. No discussion of this activity is necessary.

Approximate Time

15 to 20 minutes for activity (at home or in class)

Classroom Organization

Small groups or individuals

Doing the Activity

This activity will be a good indicator of how well students remember how to use the basic numeric facts relating standard deviation to normal distributions. If they seem clear about these ideas, no whole-class discussion will be necessary.

If groups are struggling with the ideas, you might pull the class together for a discussion of Question 1 and then have groups work on Questions 2 and 3.

Discussing and Debriefing the Activity

No discussion of this activity will likely be necessary.

Means and More in Middletown

Intent

Students get more practice dealing with the "tails" of a normal distribution and using the percentages related to intervals around the mean of one or two standard deviations.

Mathematics

Students apply the probabilities for intervals of one and two standard deviations about the mean for normal distributions.

Progression

Students examine standard deviation in three contexts and then consider whether the assumption of a normal distribution is reasonable in each instance. The subsequent discussion uses diagrams to clarify probabilities for "one-tail" areas.

Approximate Time

30 to 35 minutes for activity (at home or in class)
10 minutes for discussion

Classroom Organization

Individuals or small groups, followed by whole-class discussion

Doing the Activity

This activity should require no introduction.

Discussing and Debriefing the Activity

Questions 1–3

Have students share their sketches and solutions for Questions 1 to 3 with the class.

Question 1 is open-ended, but students are likely to make statements like these:

- About 68% of renters pay between $500 and $800.
- About 95% of renters pay between $350 and $950.
- About 16% of renters pay more than $800.

Have students explain these results with reference to a normal curve. For instance, an explanation for the first statement might use a diagram like this:

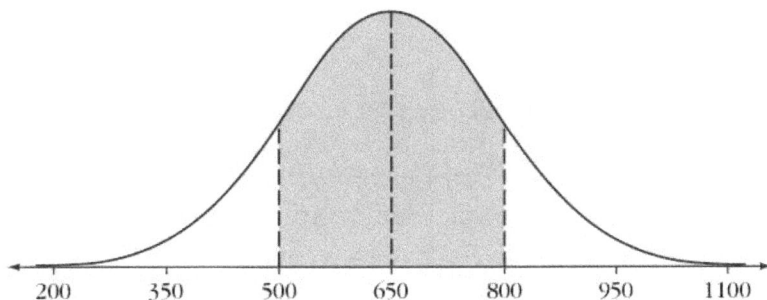

For Questions 2 and 3, students will need to do a bit of manipulation using the values 68% and 95%. After an initial presentation, ask if anyone solved a given problem in different ways. If so, have additional presentations so students can see the variety of ways there are to solve these types of problems.

For instance, for Question 3, students should reason that they want those members whose running distance is represented by the shaded area in this diagram, in which the right-hand boundary is one standard deviation above the mean:

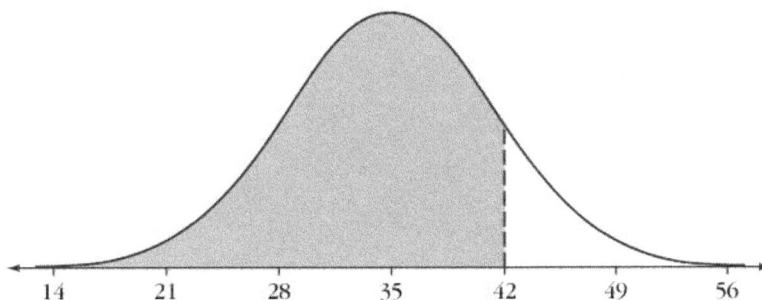

Students might find this area by noting that 68% of the members run within one standard deviation of the mean (between 28 and 42 miles) and that half of the remaining 32% run less than the amount that is one standard deviation below the mean (below 28 miles). This gives 68% + 16% = 84% who run at most one standard deviation above the mean.

A second approach is to reason that 32% of the runners have a distance more than one standard deviation from the mean, and half of these run more than one standard deviation above the mean, so those runners who run at most one standard deviation above the mean form 100% − 16% = 84% of the total.

Question 4

Have students share ideas about whether the situations in Questions 1 to 3 seem appropriate for use of a normal distribution. Of course, none will fit this distribution perfectly, because they are discrete rather than continuous distributions, but any of them might be roughly normal. In particular, many standardized tests are designed to yield roughly normal distributions of results.

Graphing Distributions

Intent

Students explore the changes in normal distribution graphs as the mean and standard deviation are changed.

Mathematics

Students compare normal curves with different means and standard deviations, using the equation of a normal curve.

Progression

Students use the graphing calculator to observe how the normal curve is affected by changing the mean or the standard deviation.

Approximate Time

25 to 35 minutes

Classroom Organization

Small groups or individuals

Doing the Activity

Before students begin graphing, you may want to point out that the equation for the normal curve involves both e and π, two very special numbers that they have encountered in other contexts.

To get them started, you may want to suggest a specific viewing window for Question 1, such as x-values from −4 to 4 and y-values from 0 to 0.4. After that, let students make their own adjustments.

Discussing and Debriefing the Activity

As students finish up, you may want to bring the class together to summarize their findings. Students have seen before that as standard deviation increases, the distribution becomes more spread out. However, seeing this graphically using an explicit function for the normal curve may give them a new perspective and solidify their understanding.

Similarly, students will probably not be surprised by what happens as the mean changes. However, seeing the distribution sliding back and forth may be dramatic enough to give them a better appreciation of what is going on.

Gifts Aren't Always Free

Intent

Students apply their knowledge of standard deviation and normal distribution to make a decision concerning car expenses.

Mathematics

Students apply the basic facts of standard deviation and normal distribution in another context.

Progression

The questions challenge students to explain the concepts of standard deviation and normal distribution as they apply to a new problem situation. The subsequent discussion sets the stage for considering probabilities for arbitrary intervals under the normal curve.

Approximate Time

25 to 30 minutes for activity (at home or in class)
10 minutes for discussion

Classroom Organization

Individuals, followed by whole-class discussion

Doing the Activity

This activity requires no introduction.

Discussing and Debriefing the Activity

Have students discuss their answers in small groups and come to a consensus on how much Craig should plan to spend each week. Then have students from several groups report.

Although students may present valid explanations that don't involve distributions, be sure to elicit explanations like those given here as well. The main purpose of this activity is to review and summarize the use of standard deviation in connection with normal distributions.

If students use 23 miles per gallon as an estimate of Craig's fuel efficiency, they will recommend that he budget about $59.78 per week. But they should point out that there is a 50% chance his costs will exceed his budget. If they don't, raise the question of how likely this.

If they use 20.5 miles per gallon (one standard deviation below average), they will recommend that Craig budget about $67.07 per week. In this case, there is only about a 16% chance that he'll go over his budget.

And if students use 18 miles per gallon (two standard deviations below average), they will recommend that Craig budget about $76.39 per week. In this case, there is only about a 2.5% chance that he'll go over his budget.

Students' answers will depend on how cautious they think Craig should be. For instance, some may feel he should play it safe and plan to spend $75. Others may suggest that he might plan on the average and then make up the shortfall some other way (such as driving less) if his car turns out to be less efficient than average.

Ask students, What should Craig do if he wants only a 10% chance of going over budget on his gasoline? They should see that Craig needs a fuel efficiency somewhere between one and two standard deviations below average. The lower the value he uses for fuel efficiency, the higher the cost estimate.

In other words, students should see that they want to make the cutoff on the normal curve so that 90% of the area is to the right of that point. But the information they have seen so far concerning normal distributions doesn't tell them precisely where to make this cutoff.

As a lead-in to the next activity, mention that we often want to know more about areas under the normal curve than simply the cases involving one or two standard deviations.

Key Question

What should Craig do if he wants only a 10% chance of going over budget on his gasoline?

Normal Areas

Intent

Students estimate areas under the normal curve.

Mathematics

Students now begin to consider the problem of determining probabilities within a normal distribution when the boundaries do not happen to fall an integer number of standard deviations from the mean. Estimating such areas will help them understand where the soon-to-be-introduced table of normal probabilities comes from.

Progression

Students estimate several areas and intervals associated with a normal curve.

Approximate Time

25 to 40 minutes

Classroom Organization

Individuals, followed by whole-class discussion

Doing the Activity

This activity should require no introduction.

Discussing and Debriefing the Activity

Have students share their estimates and methods of finding them. For Question 1, they should see that the area between $x = -0.5$ and $x = 0.5$ is more than half of the area between $x = -1$ and $x = 1$, so their estimate should be more than 34%. Tell them that careful computation shows that this area actually is approximately 38% of the total.

Although most students will probably "eyeball" the areas, you may want to ask, What's a more precise way to estimate the areas than just "eyeballing" them? They might suggest using a grid overlay or a series of rectangles to approximate the areas. If they suggest using rectangles, ask, Might a different shape (such as a trapezoid) fit the curve better than a rectangle?

Emphasize that the percentages from this activity apply to every normal distribution in terms of the standard deviation.

Key Questions

What's a more precise way to estimate the areas than just "eyeballing" them?
Might a different shape (such as a trapezoid) fit the curve better than a rectangle?

Reference: The Normal Table

Intent

These pages introduce students to a table for areas associated with the normal distribution.

Mathematics

Students examine a table that provides the area under a region of the normal curve symmetrical about the mean as a function of the number of standard deviations the area's boundaries lie from the mean.

Progression

The class discusses the table in the reference pages. The discussion emphasizes that z represents the number of standard deviations from the mean and that the region must be symmetrical about the mean. Numeric integration on the calculator is also introduced.

Approximate Time

15 to 20 minutes

Classroom Organization

Whole-class discussion

Doing the Activity

Have student volunteers read the text on the reference pages aloud. Then discuss how the table works and how it relates to the activity *Normal Areas*. Have students compare their estimates from that activity with the values in the table. Be sure they understand that z represents the *number* of standard deviations a value is from the mean, not the standard deviation itself.

For example, students should have found an estimate somewhat over 34% for the area between $x = -0.5$ and $x = 0.5$. They should see that the table value corresponding to $z = 0.5$ is .3829.

Point out that the cases $z = 1$ and $z = 2$ contain the information students have already seen, concerning the cases of one and two standard deviations. Mention that the values corresponding to these two cases are perhaps worth memorizing, because they are referred to often. Students can think of the interval within one standard deviation of the mean as containing roughly $\frac{2}{3}$ of the results (the table gives .6827) and remember that the interval within two standard deviations of the mean contains about 95% of the results. (The value of 95% corresponds more precisely to the area within about 1.96 standard deviations of the mean in each direction.)

Numeric Integration on the Calculator

Graphing calculators can find areas by numeric integration, and students may gain insight by using this feature, especially if the calculator shades the area under consideration. You might explain the idea of integration intuitively simply as "finding the area under the curve between two x-values," without discussing the connection between integration and differentiation.

Have students enter the equation for the standard normal curve (given in *Normal Areas*) and then use the integration option. The calculator will likely ask them to specify lower and upper bounds for the integral.

For instance, by giving bounds of –1 and 1, students should get the value .6827 shown in the table for the area within one standard deviation of the mean. Be sure they see that the result of .6827 corresponds to $z = 1$ in the table.

Help students see that the numeric integration feature can be used even if the interval is not symmetric about the mean. For instance, to get the probability of a result that is between two standard deviations below the mean and three standard deviations above the mean, they would use a lower bound of –2 and an upper bound of 3. Discuss how to get this value (approximately .976) from the table.

Note: Because very little of the area lies more than four standard deviations from the mean, using a lower bound of –4 or an upper bound of 4 gives an excellent approximation of the area that includes the entire "tail."

Mention that the process of finding the area under curves is an important part of calculus called *integration*. They will study this idea in the next unit, *How Much? How Fast?*

Optional: "Distributions" on the Calculator

Some graphing calculators have an option that gives specific information about various probability distributions, including the normal distribution. Again, students will need to specify the boundaries within which they want to find the probability. (*Note:* The calculator is likely to have both a "cumulative" probability feature and a probability "density" feature. In this context, students want the cumulative probability.)

In addition, the calculator may have an "inverse normal" feature. This allows the user to input a specific probability and get the upper limit for the portion of the distribution that has that probability, taking −∞ as the lower limit. For instance, if the input is .841, the output will be approximately 1, because roughly 84.1% of all results are below the value that is one standard deviation above the mean.

More Middletown Musings

Intent

Students apply the detailed data set in *The Normal Table* to the three contexts from *Means and More in Middletown.*

Mathematics

Students use the normal table to determine areas under the normal curve.

Progression

Students analyze three situations using data from the table in *The Normal Table*. The subsequent discussion emphasizes the importance of using diagrams to visualize problems and explain reasoning. Students also share ideas about finding in-between values from the table.

Approximate Time

30 minutes for activity (at home or in class)
15 minutes for discussion

Classroom Organization

Individuals, followed by whole-class discussion

Doing the Activity

The activity does not explicitly ask students to sketch normal curves. However, you may want to request labeled diagrams, which will help students to see how the various areas fit the situations and to explain their work.

Discussing and Debriefing the Activity

Question 1

Question 1 is the simplest, as it concerns an area symmetric about the mean. The associated z-value is 0.8, because the range of values goes from $120 below the mean to $120 above the mean, and 120 is 0.8 times the standard deviation of $150. The table shows that the probability associated with $z = 0.8$ is .5763, so approximately 58% of renters pay between $530 and $670 per month.

Question 2

In Question 2, students need to find the probability of a test result that is at least 2.4 standard deviations above the mean. They likely will begin by finding that the area *within* 2.4 standard deviations of the mean is .9836; this is the probability in the table associated with $z = 2.4$. Thus, the area outside this interval is .0164, and the answer to Question 2 is half of this, or .0082. In other words, about 0.82% (less than 1%) of those taking the test will score at or above 306.

Question 3

For Question 3, the relevant z-value is $\frac{5}{7}$ (approximately 0.714), because 40 miles is 5 miles above the mean, and the standard deviation is 7 miles. Because this z-value is not in the table, students will probably look at the probability associated with $z = 0.7$, which is .5161, and the probability associated with $z = 0.8$, which is .5763, and use a value between .5161 and .5763 as the probability that goes with $z = 0.714$.

Ask for ideas about how to get this in-between probability. How can you get an in-between value for the table? Students should intuitively realize that the desired probability is closer to .5161 than to .5763 (because 0.714 is closer to 0.7 than to 0.8).

The probability associated with a z-value of 0.714 is roughly .525, but proceed with Question 3 using any reasonable estimate between .5161 and .5763. (*Note: Gaps in the Table* presents a standard method for this type of estimation called *linear interpolation*. In this approach, the probability associated with $z = 0.714$ is estimated as "14% of the way" from .5161 to .5763, because 0.714 is "14% of the way" from 0.7 to 0.8. This gives roughly .5245.)

Question 3, like Question 2, involves the right-hand tail of the normal curve. Once students find the probability associated with the z-value, they subtract that probability from 1 and take half the difference. If they use .525 as the probability associated with $z = \frac{5}{7}$, they will get .2375. So, roughly 24% of the club members run 40 miles or more.

Key Question

How can you get an in-between value for the table?

Back to the Circus

Intent

Students continue to use the normal table.

Mathematics

Students analyze another problem involving the normal distribution, standard deviation, and the use of the table from *A Normal Table*.

Progression

Students examine another situation involving the normal distribution. The follow-up discussion reviews the general approach to using the normal distribution and standard deviation.

Approximate Time

35 minutes

Classroom Organization

Small groups or individuals, followed by whole-class discussion

Doing the Activity

This activity requires no introduction.

Discussing and Debriefing the Activity

Have a student present the problem. Students should see that the performer's stopping distance should represent a point on the curve so that the right-hand tail of the curve beyond that point has area .05.

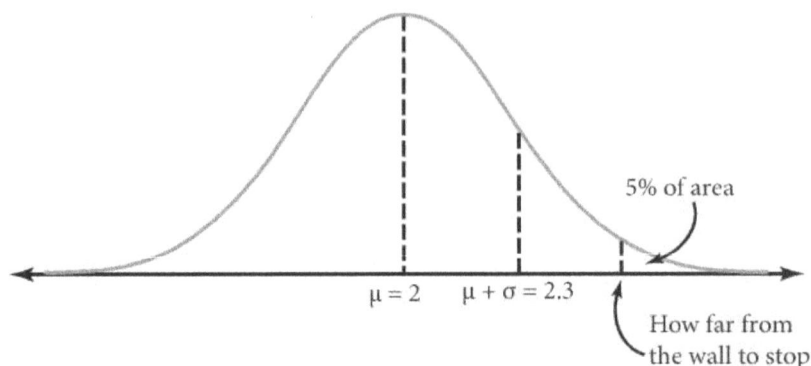

This means that the two tails together have an area of .10, so the symmetric section of the curve extending out to that point has an area of .90. In other words, students need to find the z-value in the table corresponding to .90, or $z \approx 1.65$.

Students should conclude that the performer should stop so that her distance from the wall is about 1.65 standard deviations above the mean, or
$2 + 1.65 \cdot 0.3 \approx 2.5$ meters.

Make sure students know what this means by asking, **What is the significance of 2.5 meters?** They should be able to explain that 95% of the performer's stops will take less than 2.5 meters. That is, if she hits the brakes 2.5 meters from the wall, she will hit the wall only about 5% of the time. (She will be going very slowly by that time, so she is unlikely to get hurt.)

Key Question

What is the significance of 2.5 meters?

Gaps in the Table

Intent

Students estimate probabilities using linear interpolation.

Mathematics

Students explore the estimation technique of linear interpolation. They can use this method in the remainder of the unit to find probabilities associated with z-values that are not listed in the normal table.

Progression

Students are introduced to and work with the technique of linear interpolation. The subsequent discussion uses graphs to clarify the concept.

Approximate Time

30 minutes for activity (at home or in class)
10 minutes for discussion

Classroom Organization

Individuals, followed by whole-class discussion

Doing the Activity

This activity needs no introduction.

Discussing and Debriefing the Activity

Questions 1 and 2

Have volunteers present Questions 1 and 2, which are fairly straightforward.

For Question 1b, students will probably find the average of the values from Question 1a (.9281 and .9545) and see that this average (.9413) is quite close to the probability associated with $z = 1.9$ (.9426), but not quite the same. For Question 2, they should see that 8^2 is close to, but different from, the average of 7^2 and 9^2.

For Question 2d, students will likely draw the graph of the equation $y = x^2$ and the line segment connecting the points (7, 49) and (9, 81), and then explain that the point on this segment with $x = 8$ is the midpoint of the segment, and its y-coordinate is 65. Bring out that the segment is slightly above the graph, which accounts for the fact that the result of linear interpolation is greater than the actual value of 8^2. The curvature in the diagram below is exaggerated to make the difference between the curve and the line more visible.

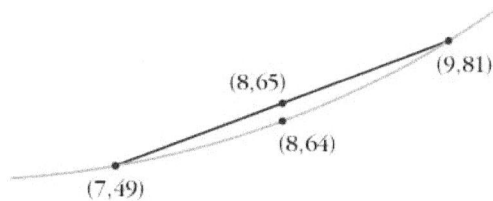

Question 3

Question 3 is intended to reveal why the technique is called *linear* interpolation. Students should see that for the linear function $g(x) = 2x - 1$, the value of $g(8)$ is, in fact, exactly halfway between $g(7)$ and $g(9)$.

Ask for an explanation of this relationship. Students might use a graph of g to point out that the midpoint of the segment connecting (7, 13) and (9, 17)—the point (8, 15)—is actually on the graph because the graph is a straight line. The fact that this point is on the graph means that $15 = g(8)$.

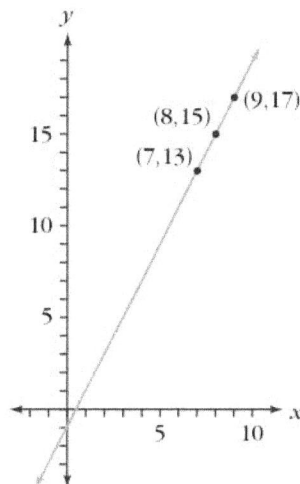

Explain that the technique is called *linear* interpolation because, in general, it is based on approximating the given portion of a graph by a line segment.

Question 4

For Question 4a, students should see that because 0.82 is one-fifth of the way from 0.8 to 0.9, the associated probability should be one-fifth of the way from .5763 to .6319, or approximately .5874. Students can find a more exact value—approximately .5878—using a calculator's numeric integration feature, as discussed in the notes for *The Normal Table*.

For Question 4b, students need to recognize that $\frac{4}{3}$ is one-third of the way from 1.3 to 1.4. If necessary, suggest they write $\frac{4}{3}$ as a decimal.

Discuss the fact that for linear functions (such as function g in Question 3), this more general form of linear interpolation continues to work perfectly. For instance, 6 is one-fifth of the way from 5 to 10, and $g(6)$, which is 11, is exactly one-fifth of the way from $g(5)$, which is 9, to $g(10)$, which is 19.

Supplemental Activity

***Generalizing Linear Interpolation* (extension)** asks students to give a general formula for how to estimate the value of a function at a point $x = c$ if they know the values at $x = a$ and $x = b$ (with $a < c < b$).

A Normal Poll

Intent

Students apply the central limit theorem to a polling situation.

Mathematics

Students learn how to use the central limit theorem to apply the normal distribution to polls. They are led to the realization that the true proportion will be the mean value for the normal distribution and are reminded of the guideline that poll size should not exceed 5% of the population.

Progression

Students use standard deviation to estimate the probability that a 50-person poll will correctly identify the leading candidate. The subsequent discussion reviews the meaning of the relevant area under the normal curve in terms of the context. It also reviews the status of the central unit problem, clarifying that students need to find out how to get the mean and standard deviation in terms of n and p.

Approximate Time

20 minutes for activity (at home or in class)
10 to 20 minutes for discussion

Classroom Organization

Small groups or individuals, followed by whole-class discussion

Doing the Activity

Begin by asking students once again, What is the connection between normal distributions and the central unit problem? Elicit a statement of the central limit theorem, which asserts that for "reasonably big" polls, the normal curve approximates the probability distribution of poll results for a given population. Students might not get any further than that, but this activity will show them how to use the central limit theorem to apply the normal distribution to polls.

Discussing and Debriefing the Activity

For Question 1, see if anyone realizes that the mean for the approximating normal distribution is the same as the proportion of the overall population that favors the candidate. If not, point this out yourself, and ask, Can anyone explain why the mean for the approximating normal distribution should be equal to the true proportion? This is saying that the average of many sample proportions should equal the true proportion. This observation should make intuitive sense to students, and you can tell them that it holds true in general.

Based on the assumptions in the problem, the presenter for Question 2 should explain that the task is to find the area under the approximating normal curve corresponding to results above .50.

To get the area above .50, students will probably first work with an area that is symmetric about the mean. The mean is .6, so they need to examine the area between .50 and .70, which is shaded in the diagram below. The tick marks on the horizontal scale correspond to the mean and to the values one, two, and three standard deviations from the mean.

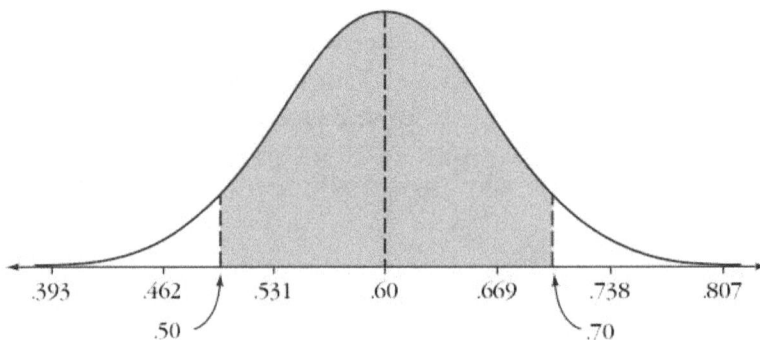

The shaded area consists of all values within .10 of the mean. But 0.10 is approximately 1.45 standard deviations (because $\frac{.10}{.069} \approx 1.45$), so students need the value in the table corresponding to $z = 1.45$. They might use linear interpolation to estimate the midpoint between the entries for $z = 1.4$ and $z = 1.5$ and get approximately .852 for the shaded area.

Here are two ways students might proceed to find the area above .50:

- As the shaded area plus the area to the right of .70 (which is the right half of the unshaded area): .852 + 0.5(1 − .852).

- As the area to the right of .60 (which is $\frac{1}{2}$ because .60 is the mean) plus the left half of the shaded area: .5 + 0.5 · .852.

Both approaches give an area of .926.

Ask, **What does it mean that this area is .926?** Students should understand that it means Harriet has about a 92.6% chance of getting a poll result showing Henry in the lead. Notice that even though Henry actually has the support of 60% of the voters (a fairly large lead), there is about a 7.4% chance that a 50-person poll will show him trailing.

Where Are We Now?

Have students discuss where they are in the process of solving the central unit problem. You might have students pair up, have one person in each pair talk for some length of time (such as two minutes) while the other listens carefully, and then have partners exchange roles. You can then move on to a whole-class discussion.

Students should see that at this stage, if they know the mean and standard deviation of the approximating normal distribution for a given poll, they can find the probability of getting any given range of results from that poll.

Basically, there are two more big steps they will need to take:

- Finding the mean and standard deviation of the normal curve that approximates the binomial distribution
- Finding the true proportion from the sample proportion

Key Questions

What is the connection between normal distributions and the central unit problem?
Why should the mean for the approximating normal distribution be equal to the true proportion?
What does it mean that this area is .926?

A Plus for the Community

Intent

This activity sets the stage for introduction of a formal definition of mean for a discrete probability distribution.

Mathematics

This activity (along with *Mean and Standard Deviation for Probability Distributions*) extends the concepts of mean and standard deviation from sets of data to probability distributions. Students see that the "large number of trials" method for computing mean and standard deviation is independent of the number of trials.

Progression

Students analyze a carnival game for the average amount the game would expect to pay out per spin if 400 people, and then 5000 people, played. Students discover that the associated probabilities are not dependent upon the number of players. This realization leads, in the subsequent discussion, to a definition of *mean* for a probability distribution. The discussion includes proving algebraically that the average is independent of the number of spins.

Approximate Time

25 minutes for activity (at home or in class)
15 minutes for discussion

Classroom Organization

Individuals, followed by whole-class discussion

Doing the Activity

This activity requires no introduction.

Discussing and Debriefing the Activity

In Question 1, students need only find the sum

$$400 \cdot \$1 + 400 \cdot \$2 + 150 \cdot \$3 + 50 \cdot \$10$$

which gives a total of $2,150, and then divide by 1000, which gives an average of $2.15 per spin.

Before going on to Question 2, ask students, What is the term for this average payoff? Use the phrase "in the long run" if necessary. Review that this long-run average is called the *expected value* per spin.

For Question 2, students may give different arguments as to why changing the number of spins doesn't change the expected value. If needed, have them write out the expressions used for the computation in the cases of 1000 spins and 5000 spins:

- For 1000 spins: $\dfrac{400 \cdot 1 + 400 \cdot 2 + 150 \cdot 3 + 50 \cdot 10}{1000}$

- For 5000 spins: $\dfrac{2000 \cdot 1 + 2000 \cdot 2 + 750 \cdot 3 + 250 \cdot 10}{5000}$

They should see that the expression for 5000 spins is the same as that for 1000 spins except that the numerator and denominator are both five times as big, so the two expressions are equivalent.

Point out that in either case, the expected value is simply the mean of the actual results. Explain that mathematicians often use the simpler term *mean*, even in the context of probability distributions, as a synonym for expected value. That is, the *mean* or *expected value* of a probability distribution is simply the numeric mean of a set of results that fit the probabilities perfectly.

Mention that in the case of a continuous distribution, such as the normal distribution, it is impossible to do this with a finite set of results. Thus, a more sophisticated definition of *mean* is needed for continuous distributions.

Help the class see that if a set of results gives a probability bar graph that is close to the normal curve, those results would have a numeric average close to the mean of the normal distribution. This is because results above the mean would average out with results below the mean.

Proving the Average Is Independent of the Number of Spins

Students have seen that 1000 spins and 5000 spins give the same average result, and they probably have an intuitive understanding of why this is so. But they should be able to prove this in general.

Ask, How can you prove that the expected value does not depend on the number of spins? If needed, suggest students use a variable for the number of spins. They may recognize immediately that the variable should "cancel out" somewhere, but have them work out the details.

What expression would give the expected value for *N* spins? This should lead the class to an expression like

$$\frac{.4N \cdot 1 + .4N \cdot 2 + .15N \cdot 3 + .05N \cdot 10}{N}$$

How can we simplify this expression? Students should be able to factor the numerator as

$$(.4 \cdot 1 + .4 \cdot 2 + .15 \cdot 3 + .05 \cdot 10)N$$

and see that the overall fraction is simply

$$.4 \cdot 1 + .4 \cdot 2 + .15 \cdot 3 + .05 \cdot 10$$

Point out that in this expression, students are simply multiplying each possible outcome by its probability. This shows that the expected value will be the same for *any* set of data that matches the probability distribution.

Mention that in most textbooks, the mean or expected value for a (discrete) probability distribution is defined by the summation equation

$$\text{mean} = \sum P(x_i) \cdot x_i$$

where the variable x_i represents the possible outcomes of the experiment and $P(x_i)$ is the probability of getting the outcome x_i. Help students see that this expression is simply the generalization of the expression

$$.4 \cdot 1 + .4 \cdot 2 + .15 \cdot 3 + .05 \cdot 10$$

Clarify that this use of the summation symbol is somewhat different from students' previous encounters with it. For instance, in the expression

$$\sum_{t=1}^{5} t$$

there is a term in the sum for each whole-number value of t from 1 through 5. In the expression $\sum P(x_i) \cdot x_i$, there is a term in the sum for each possible outcome, and these outcomes can be any set of values, not necessarily integers.

In this activity's situation, there were four outcomes for the spinner: 1, 2, 3, and 10. We might label these four outcomes as x_1, x_2, x_3, and x_4, but the subscripts 1 through 4 are not the same as the outcomes themselves. It's coincidental that the first three outcomes—1, 2, and 3—happen to match their subscripts.

Key Questions

What is the term for this average payoff?
How can you prove that the expected value does not depend on the number of spins?
What expression would give the expected value for N spins?

Means and Standard Deviations

Intent

In these activities, students develop formulas for the mean and standard deviation of the theoretical distribution of poll results.

Mathematics

These activities look at how to relate the parameters of mean and standard deviation to the size of a poll and to the true proportion for the population from which the sample is taken.

Progression

The reference material *Mean and Standard Deviation for Probability Distributions* extends the concept of standard deviation to probability distributions, and students apply that knowledge in *A Distribution Example*. In *The Search Is On!*, students develop formulas for the mean and standard deviation of a probability distribution of poll results. They try these new formulas out in *Putting Your Formulas to Work*. The formulas are then further adapted for obtaining the mean and standard deviation of sample proportions, in *From Numbers to Proportions*. In *Is Twice as Many Twice as Good?*, students use their refined formulas to explore the effect of poll size on the standard deviation of poll results.

Reference: Mean and Standard Deviation for Probability Distributions
A Distribution Example
The Search Is On!
Why Is That Batter Sneezing?
Putting Your Formulas to Work
From Numbers to Proportions
Is Twice as Many Twice as Good?

Reference: Mean and Standard Deviation for Probability Distributions

Intent

These pages review the steps for computing mean and standard deviation and applying these concepts to probability distributions.

Mathematics

This material extends the concept of standard deviation from sets of data to probability distributions. It introduces the "probability method" for computing mean and standard deviation for a probability distribution and introduces the concept of **variance**. In the discussion, students algebraically prove, as they did for mean in *A Plus for the Community*, that the standard deviation of a probability distribution is independent of the number of trials.

Progression

The teacher introduces this reference material with a discussion that defines standard deviation for a discrete probability distribution. The class reviews the steps for computing standard deviation. Students verify that for data sets fitting a discrete probability distribution, the standard deviation is independent of the size of the data set. Variance is defined as the square of the standard deviation.

Approximate Time

35 minutes

Classroom Organization

Whole-class discussion

Doing the Activity

Remind students that there are two crucial parameters for a normal distribution: mean and standard deviation. Point out that they have seen that the term *mean,* as just defined in the discussion of *A Plus for the Community*, is an extension of the same concept for sets of data. The next task is to extend the concept of standard deviation to probability distributions.

Ask students to review how to compute σ for a finite set of data. How do you compute standard deviation for a finite set of data? Go over the steps as needed:

a.   Find the mean of the *N* data items.
b.   Find the square of the difference between each data item and the mean.
c.   Add the squared differences.
d.   Divide by *N*.
e.   Take the square root of this quotient.

How can you use these steps to represent σ, in general, using summation notation? If students use μ for the result of step a (the mean) and $x_1, x_2 \ldots, x_N$ as the data items, they should get the equation

$$\sigma = \sqrt{\frac{\sum\limits_{i=1}^{N} (x_i - \mu)^2}{N}}$$

Using Outcomes that Fit a Probability Distribution

Tell students to imagine a set of results that perfectly fits the probabilities for the spinner from *A Plus for the Community*. Then ask, Would the standard deviation for that data set depend on the number of spins? They will probably guess that like the mean, the standard deviation is independent of the number of spins.

Why should the standard deviation be independent of the number of spins? Students might give an intuitive explanation such as, "If you double the number of spins, you have twice as many terms in the numerator and twice as big a denominator, so the fraction is the same."

You may want to have students write out an expression for the standard deviation for data sets fitting the spinner, perhaps having half the class do the case of four hundred 1s, four hundred 2s, one hundred fifty 3s, and fifty 10s, and the other half do the case of two thousand 1s, two thousand 2s, seven hundred fifty 3s, and two hundred fifty 10s. They don't need to do the arithmetic, but should simply write out an expression for the standard deviation. Remind students that they found that the mean of either data set is 2.15, so they can use that in their expressions.

They should get these expressions and should see (without actually carrying out the computations) that they are equal:

$$\sqrt{\frac{400 \cdot (1-2.15)^2 + 400 \cdot (2-2.15)^2 + 150 \cdot (3-2.15)^2 + 50 \cdot (10-2.15)^2}{1000}}$$

$$\sqrt{\frac{2000 \cdot (1-2.15)^2 + 2000 \cdot (2-2.15)^2 + 750 \cdot (3-2.15)^2 + 250 \cdot (10-2.15)^2}{5000}}$$

Proving Standard Deviation Is Independent of the Number of Spins

Now ask, **How can you prove the standard deviation is independent of the number of spins?** Because students earlier replaced 1000 and 5000 with N for the mean, they will likely suggest doing that here. This gives the expression

$$\sqrt{\frac{.4N \cdot (1-2.15)^2 + .4N \cdot (2-2.15)^2 + .15N \cdot (3-2.15)^2 + .05N \cdot (10-2.15)^2}{N}}$$

By factoring out N, this simplifies to

$$\sqrt{.4 \cdot (1-2.15)^2 + .4 \cdot (2-2.15)^2 + .15 \cdot (3-2.15)^2 + .05 \cdot (10-2.15)^2}$$

If they haven't already done so for the earlier expressions, have students find the value of this expression. This gives $\sigma = 1.93$.

Ask, **How can we generalize this expression to an arbitrary discrete probability distribution?** As with the mean, students should use the variable x_i to represent the possible outcomes of the experiment, $P(x_i)$ for the probability of getting the outcome x_i, and μ to represent the mean, which produces this equation:

$$\sigma = \sqrt{\sum P(x_i) \cdot (x_i - \mu)^2}$$

Mention that statistics textbooks typically use this expression to state the definition of standard deviation for discrete probability distributions. But students generally can use the "large number of trials" approach as a more intuitive way to perform the calculation.

You might also mention that as with the mean, a more sophisticated approach is needed for continuous distributions. However, the formal definition here is consistent with what students have seen involving the normal distribution.

Variance

Tell students that for a data set $x_1, x_2, \ldots, x_N$, with mean μ, the expression

$$\frac{\sum_{i=1}^{N} (x_i - \mu)^2}{N}$$

is called the **variance** of the set of data. Thus, the variance is simply the square of the standard deviation and is often represented simply as σ^2. Explain that in some contexts, it's easier to work with the variance than with the standard deviation. (Students will do that in *The Search Is On!*)

The variance can be expressed using probabilities by the expression

$$\sum P(x_i) \cdot (x_i - \mu)^2$$

Note: Technically, *mean* and *expected value* are not synonymous. Statisticians speak of "the mean of a distribution" but "the expected value of a random variable" having that distribution. But the mean and the expected value are numerically identical, and the distinction is not important in the context in which students are working.

Key Questions

How do you compute standard deviation for a finite set of data?

How can you represent σ, in general, using summation notation?

Would the standard deviation for a data set that fits the spinner probabilities depend on the number of spins?

Why should the standard deviation be independent of the number of spins?

How can you prove the standard deviation is independent of the number of spins?

How can we generalize this expression to an arbitrary discrete probability distribution?

A Distribution Example

Intent

Students solidify their understanding of the meaning of *mean* and *standard deviation* for probability distributions, as well as gain experience using the "probability method."

Mathematics

Students practice using the "probability method" to calculate the mean and standard deviation of a probability distribution and consider why this gives the same result as the "large number of trials" approach.

Progression

Students find the mean and standard deviation for a simple data set that fits a given probability distribution. They then calculate both values again, using the probability method, and explain why the results are the same.

Approximate Time

30 minutes for activity (at home or in class)
10 to 15 minutes for discussion

Classroom Organization

Individuals, followed by whole-class discussion

Doing the Activity

This activity requires no introduction.

Discussing and Debriefing the Activity

In reviewing this activity, focus first on the mean, discussing Questions 1, 3, and 4. Then turn to Questions 2, 5, and 6, which involve standard deviation.

Students might suggest finding the mean and standard deviation for the data set by entering the data items in a calculator and having the calculator do the computation. For this discussion, however, it's essential that they see how the arithmetic works.

Questions 1, 3, and 4

Ask a volunteer to answer this question: **What arithmetic expression could you use to get the answer to Question 1?** Students are likely to use an expression like

$$\frac{1\cdot0+3\cdot1+3\cdot2+1\cdot3}{8}$$

to find this mean. If someone suggests $\frac{0+1+1+1+2+2+2+3}{8}$ instead, it will help for the discussion of Question 4 to have students rework this into the other form.

What expression could you use for Question 3? The expression will likely look like this:

$$\frac{1}{8}\cdot0+\frac{3}{8}\cdot1+\frac{3}{8}\cdot2+\frac{1}{8}\cdot3$$

This may be the first time some students have used the "probability method," so be sure they understand the computational process.

Bring out the role of the distributive property in seeing why the two expressions give the same result. You might use this sequence of equations:

$$\frac{1\cdot0+3\cdot1+3\cdot2+1\cdot3}{8}=\frac{1}{8}(1\cdot0+3\cdot1+3\cdot2+1\cdot3)$$

$$=\frac{1}{8}\cdot1\cdot0+\frac{1}{8}\cdot3\cdot1+\frac{1}{8}\cdot3\cdot2+\frac{1}{8}\cdot1\cdot3$$

$$=\frac{1}{8}\cdot0+\frac{3}{8}\cdot1+\frac{3}{8}\cdot2+\frac{1}{8}\cdot3$$

To clarify the connection, you might have students focus on a specific term in the final expression. For instance, in the term $\frac{3}{8}\cdot2$, we are multiplying the outcome 2 by its probability $\frac{3}{8}$. Bring out that the coefficient $\frac{3}{8}$ is the ratio of 3 and 8, where 3 is the coefficient of the outcome 2 in the expression $\frac{1\cdot0+3\cdot1+3\cdot2+1\cdot3}{8}$ and 8 is the denominator of that expression.

You might also look at an example of a different data set that fits the probabilities, such as two 0s, six 1s, six 2s, and two 3s, to see why this gives the same mean as the original set.

Ask, **How can the experiment of flipping three coins and counting the number of heads have a mean of 1.5, when you can never get $1\frac{1}{2}$ heads?**

Students should be able to say that given a large number of trials, the number of heads should average out to half of the number of coins flipped, or an average of $1\frac{1}{2}$ heads per 3-coin trial. This interpretation of mean helps make the connection between the data-set approach and the probability approach.

Questions 2, 5, and 6

For Question 2, students are likely to use an expression like

$$\sqrt{\frac{1 \cdot (0-1.5)^2 + 3 \cdot (1-1.5)^2 + 3 \cdot (2-1.5)^2 + 1 \cdot (3-1.5)^2}{8}}$$

For Question 5, the computation will look like this:

$$\sqrt{\frac{1}{8} \cdot (0-1.5)^2 + \frac{3}{8} \cdot (1-1.5)^2 + \frac{3}{8} \cdot (2-1.5)^2 + \frac{1}{8} \cdot (3-1.5)^2}$$

Help students see that although the two computations are a bit more complex than in Questions 1 and 3, the distributive property still explains why they give the same result.

Key Questions

What arithmetic expression could you use to get the answer to Question 1?
What expression could you use for Question 3?
How can the experiment of flipping three coins and counting the number of heads have a mean of 1.5, when you can never get $1\frac{1}{2}$ heads?

The Search Is On!

Intent

Students look for formulas for the mean and standard deviation of poll results in terms of the poll size and the true population.

Mathematics

Students work with specific cases to find formulas for the mean and standard deviation of poll results.

Progression

Students find the means and variances for probability distributions for polls with specific values of p and n and then look for patterns. The class works through one example together and develops a plan for organizing the information, which is used to develop formulas for the mean and the standard deviation. They then apply the formulas to the situations from *Why Is That Batter Sneezing?*

Approximate Time

75 to 80 minutes

Classroom Organization

Small groups, followed by whole-class discussion

Doing the Activity

Introduce this activity by reminding students that *mean* and *standard deviation* play a key role in the normal distribution that approximates poll results. In this activity, they will actually find the mean and standard deviation for the appropriate binomial distribution and then use these values as the mean and standard deviation for the approximating normal distribution.

Ask, **What does the probability distribution for poll results depend on?** Review that there are two parameters:

- n, the size of the poll
- p, the fraction of the overall population that supports the candidate

Remind students that we often express p, the true proportion, as a percentage. Explain that the goal of this activity is to find the mean and standard deviation for the probability distribution of poll results—that is, of the binomial distribution—in terms of these two parameters.

Ask for suggestions on how to proceed. **How might you find the mean and standard deviation in terms of these two parameters?** Broadly speaking, the approach will be to gather information about specific cases and look for patterns. However, several things will make this process easier. Build on students' ideas when possible, but tell them that the following suggestions (included in the activity) will make it easier to see a pattern in their results:

- Work with the *number* of votes the candidate gets in the poll, rather than the proportion. (Once students have a general formula based on the number of votes, they will convert the formula to one based on the proportion of votes. See *From Numbers to Proportions*.)
- Find a formula for the *variance* rather than for the standard deviation.
- Start with a particular value for p and various values of n, and get formulas for the mean and variance, for that value of p, in terms of n.

Once students find formulas for μ and σ^2 for a particular value of p, they can try a different value of p and get formulas for this new value of p. Eventually they should get a general formula for both the mean and variance in terms of n and p. They can then get a general formula for standard deviation by putting their formula for the variance under a square-root sign.

Getting Started

We recommend that as a class, you work through a specific value of p (the true proportion) using several consecutive values of n (the poll size). For instance, suppose $p = .4$, and start with the case $n = 3$.

What are the mean and variance if $n = 3$ and $p = .4$? Help students see that they need to find the probability of getting each possible poll result—no votes for the candidate, 1 vote for the candidate, and so on. Review the use of combinatorial coefficients as needed.

Here are expressions and values for each possibility:
- $P(0 \text{ "yes" votes}) = {}_3C_0 \cdot .4^0 \cdot .6^3 = .216$
- $P(1 \text{ "yes" vote}) = {}_3C_1 \cdot .4^1 \cdot .6^2 = .432$
- $P(2 \text{ "yes" votes}) = {}_3C_2 \cdot .4^2 \cdot .6^1 = .288$
- $P(3 \text{ "yes" votes}) = {}_3C_3 \cdot .4^3 \cdot .6^0 = .064$

Ask students, **What should be true about these four probabilities?** Bring out that they can check their work by verifying that the probabilities add up to 1. (*Caution:* For larger values of n, students need to be aware that round-off errors may give slightly incorrect results and a sum slightly different from 1.)

Once students have the probabilities, they can use either the "large number of trials" approach or the "probability method" for calculating mean and variance. Bring the class together to discuss the value of the mean as soon as students seem ready, as they will need the correct value to find the variance.

Be careful not to let students get so lost in the computations that they lose sight of the overall picture, perhaps by asking questions like these: What does n represent? Where did the number .4 come from? What do these probabilities mean?

If students use the "large number of trials" method, they might assume, for instance, that they had taken 1000 polls of size 3 and the results were distributed exactly as the theory predicts. Thus, they would have 216 polls with no "yes" votes, 432 polls with 1 "yes" vote, 288 polls with 2 "yes" votes, and 64 polls with 3 "yes" votes. They would find the average number of "yes" votes per poll by the expression $\dfrac{216 \cdot 0 + 432 \cdot 1 + 288 \cdot 2 + 64 \cdot 3}{1000}$, which is 1.2.

If they use the "probability method," they would find the mean by the expression $.216 \cdot 0 + .432 \cdot 1 + .288 \cdot 2 + .064 \cdot 3$, which is also 1.2.

For the variance, if students use the set of 1000 polls just described, they should see that polls with no "yes" votes are each 1.2 from the mean; those with 1 "yes" vote are 0.2 from the mean; those with 2 "yes" votes are 0.8 from the mean; and those with 3 "yes" votes are 1.8 from the mean. Therefore, the variance is

$$\frac{216(1.2)^2 + 432(0.2)^2 + 288(0.8)^2 + 64(1.8)^2}{1000} = 0.72$$

If they use the "probability method," they would find the variance by the expression $.216(1.2)^2 + .432(0.2)^2 + .288(0.8)^2 + .064(1.8)^2$.

Once students have found the values of μ and σ^2 for this case, have them set up a plan for organizing their information. For instance, they might use a table like this:

Results for $p = .4$		
n	Mean	Variance
3	1.2	.72

Continuing with Other Values of n

Once this case is completed, continue with other values of n. Although the case $n = 1$ is somewhat artificial as a poll size, the mechanics of the analysis are simple, and this case is very useful in helping students see the pattern.

Here is a summary of the mechanics for $n = 1$ and $n = 2$, using the "probability method":

For $n = 1$:

- $P(0$ "yes" votes$) = .6$
- $P(1$ "yes" vote$) = .4$

Mean $= .6 \cdot 0 + .4 \cdot 1 = .4$

Variance $= .6(0 - .4)^2 + .4(1 - .4)^2 = .24$

For $n = 2$:

- $P(0$ "yes" votes$) = .6^2$
- $P(1$ "yes" vote$) = 2 \cdot .6 \cdot .4$
- $P(2$ "yes" votes$) = .4^2$

Mean $= .6^2 \cdot 0 + 2 \cdot .6 \cdot .4 \cdot 1 + .4^2 \cdot 2 = .8$

Variance $= .6^2(0 - .8)^2 + 2 \cdot .6 \cdot .4(1 - .8)^2 + .4^2(2 - .8)^2 = .48$

Putting these values into the table gives this information about the case $p = .4$:

Results for $p = .4$		
n	Mean	Variance
1	.4	.24
2	.8	.48
3	1.2	.72

At this point, you might ask, **Do you see any patterns or formulas for this value of p?** Students are likely to be able to find formulas for the mean and variance in terms of n. Specifically, they should see that the mean is $.4n$ and the variance is $.24n$. They may want to do another case to confirm the pattern.

Examining Other Values of p

Once the class has found formulas for $p = .4$, let groups work on finding similar formulas for other values of p. Then have them look for general formulas for the mean and standard deviation in terms of n and p.

Some groups may be able to guess the general formulas just from this example or at least see that the mean is simply np. It is somewhat more difficult to see that the variance is $np(1 - p)$. But even if groups see the general pattern from data for a single value of p, urge them to examine another value of p to confirm the pattern.

You might want to offer assistance once a group has found formulas for other specific values of *p*. For instance, if a group has seen that the variance is .24*n* when *p* = .4 and is .21*n* when *p* = .7, you might ask how they could get the coefficient .24 for the case *p* = .4 and .21 for the case *p* = .7.

Reminder: As *n* increases, the temptation to round off the probabilities becomes greater, so it's important that students realize that values found after rounding off may not fit the formula perfectly.

As they finish, ask some groups to prepare to present their work. Because all groups should ultimately find the same formulas, focus the presentations on *how* they found them.

Discussing and Debriefing the Activity

The Intuitive Meaning of the Formula for the Mean

After, or perhaps during, the presentations, ask, Why does the formula $\mu = np$ make intuitive sense?

You might want to work through an example. For instance, ask, If you poll 1000 people from a much larger population with a true proportion of .6, how many "yes" votes would you expect on the average? Students should reason that if 60% of the overall population are "yes" voters, then about 600 polled voters should be "yes" voters. Help them see that although any given poll might have a different result, the average result should be 600. The goal is to connect the formal computation of the mean to this intuitive meaning of "expected value."

Formulas for Variance and Standard Deviation

Students should get the formula $\sigma^2 = np(1 - p)$ for the variance. They then simply take the square root to get the formula for the standard deviation, $\sigma = \sqrt{np(1 - p)}$. (Many books use the symbol *q* in place of 1 − *p*, so that the formula for standard deviation is simply $\sigma = \sqrt{npq}$ and the general expression for binomial probabilities is $_nC_r \cdot p^r \cdot q^{n-r}$.)

Ask, What is the standard deviation if *p* is 0 or 1? Why does this make sense? Students should see that both of these extreme cases give $\sigma = 0$. This makes sense because in these cases, the voters all agree, and there cannot be any variation from one poll to the next.

Post the formulas for the mean and standard deviation:

For the binomial distribution with *n* trials and probability *p* of success for each trial, the mean and standard deviation for the number of successes are given by these formulas:

$$\mu = np$$
$$\sigma = \sqrt{np(1-p)}$$

You might also post a statement about how these formulas apply to polling:

If a poll is done using sampling with replacement, then *np* and $\sqrt{np(1-p)}$ are the mean and standard deviation for the number of "yes" votes in an *n*-person poll in which the true proportion is *p*.

Point out that students have not proved these formulas; they have only found patterns based on specific cases. Assure them, however, that these formulas can be proved in general.

Applying the Formulas to the Situations from *Why Is That Batter Sneezing?*

If students have not yet completed and discussed *Why Is That Batter Sneezing?*, this portion of the discussion should be delayed until after they have done so. For your convenience, these notes are duplicated in the discussion notes for that activity.

Ask students, How could you apply the formulas from *The Search Is On!* to the situations in *Why Is That Batter Sneezing?*

For example, have them imagine that the batter from Question 1 will come to bat 200 more times this season. They should continue to assume that every time he bats, he has a 40% chance of getting a hit.

How many hits would you expect him to get? Students' intuition should suggest 40% of 200, or 80 hits. Point out that this is precisely what the formula $\mu = np$ says.

How much variation is likely in the number of hits he gets? Specifically, what is the standard deviation for the number of hits? You may want to let students work on this in their groups. They should see that they simply need to apply the formula $\sigma = \sqrt{np(1-p)}$ to get that the standard deviation of his number of hits is $\sqrt{200 \cdot .4 \cdot .6}$, or approximately 6.9.

What does this standard deviation tell you? Students might say the batter has about a 68% chance of getting between 73 and 87 hits or about a 95% chance of getting between 66 and 94 hits.

As time allows, you might do a similar analysis of the situation from Question 2 or of some of the situations students created for Question 3.

Key Questions

What does the probability distribution for poll results depend on?
How might you find the mean and standard deviation in terms of these two parameters?
What are the mean and variance if $n = 3$ and $p = .4$?
Do you see any patterns or formulas for this value of p?
Why does the formula $\mu = np$ make intuitive sense?
If you poll 1000 people from a much larger population with a true proportion of .6, how many "yes" votes would you expect on the average?
What is the standard deviation if p is 0 or 1? Why does this make sense?
How could you apply these formulas to the situations from *Why Is That Batter Sneezing?*
How many hits would you expect him to get?
How much variation is likely in the number of hits he gets? What's the standard deviation?
What does this standard deviation tell you?

Supplemental Activity

Another View of the Central Limit Theorem **(reinforcement or extension)**
asks students to consider mean and standard deviation as they examine a case of the central limit theorem in which the original distribution is not binomial.

Why Is That Batter Sneezing?

Intent

Students consider a wider range of applications for binomial probabilities.

Mathematics

Students review the key ideas of the binomial distribution in new contexts.

Progression

Students examine two new situations involving a binomial distribution and then create their own. In the follow-up discussion, students apply what they learned in *The Search Is On!* to the situations from this activity.

Approximate Time

30 minutes for activity (at home or in class)
10 to 15 minutes for discussion

Classroom Organization

Individuals, then groups, followed by whole-class discussion

Doing the Activity

Little or no introduction is required.

Discussing and Debriefing the Activity

Ask students to come to agreement in their groups on answers to Questions 1 and 2 and to choose the best of their situations from Question 3. Then have several students report on Questions 1 and 2a through 2c, which are fairly straightforward applications of the ideas students have been using throughout the unit.

Here are graphs for Questions 1b and 2c:

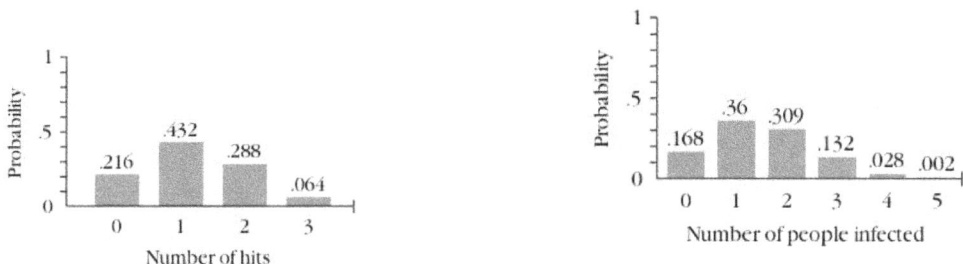

Let students share their ideas about Question 2d, which may vary. If Alida is at the most contagious stage of the flu, it's unlikely that no one will become infected. But the probability is not so small to rule out the possibility that she is at that stage.

Key Components for the Binomial Distribution

Use the discussion of Questions 1 and 2 to review the key elements that are required for a situation to fit the binomial distribution:

- The situation involves repetition of some "experiment" that has two possible outcomes.
- Each repetition is independent.

For example, the experiment could be "polling a voter," "having a turn at bat," or "exposing someone to the flu." "Independent" means the results of one experiment do not affect the probabilities for the next experiment. For instance, if a batter does not get a hit his first time at bat, he is assumed to still have a .4 probability of getting a hit the next time.

Now ask each group to present its most interesting binomial situation for Question 3. Make sure the situation truly represents the binomial distribution—that is, involves the key components discussed above.

Applying the Formulas from The Search Is On!

Ask students, **How could you apply the formulas from *The Search Is On!* to the situations from this activity?**

For example, have them imagine that the batter from Question 1 will come to bat 200 more times this season. They should continue to assume that every time he bats, he has a 40% chance of getting a hit.

How many hits would you expect him to get? Students' intuition should suggest 40% of 200, or 80 hits. Point out that this is precisely what the formula $\mu = np$ says.

How much variation is likely in the number of hits he gets? Specifically, what is the standard deviation for the number of hits? You may want to let students work on this in their groups. They should see that they simply need to apply the formula $\sigma = \sqrt{np(1-p)}$ to get that the standard deviation of his number of hits is $\sqrt{200 \cdot .4 \cdot .6}$, or approximately 6.9.

What does this standard deviation tell you? Students might say the batter has about a 68% chance of getting between 73 and 87 hits or about a 95% chance of getting between 66 and 94 hits.

As time allows, you might do a similar analysis of the situation from Question 2 or of some of the situations students created for Question 3.

Key Questions

How could you apply the formulas from *The Search Is On!* to the situations from this activity?

How many hits would you expect him to get?

How much variation is likely in the number of hits he gets? What's the standard deviation for the number of hits?

What does this standard deviation tell you?

Putting Your Formulas to Work

Intent

Students apply the formulas they developed in *The Search Is On!*

Mathematics

In this activity, students apply the formulas for the mean and standard deviation of the theoretical distribution for poll results. They also ponder the seeming paradox that while larger polls should give more accurate results, the formula for standard deviation in this context yields a larger standard deviation for bigger polls.

Progression

Students first find the probability that a poll will show a particular candidate in the lead, given n and p. They are then asked to explain the fact that as poll sizes increase, so does the standard deviation. They should conclude that although the variation in the number of votes goes up as n increases, the variation in the proportion of votes goes down. This will motivate the need to find formulas for the distribution of sample proportions that come from a poll, which students will do in *From Numbers to Proportions*.

Approximate Time

25 to 30 minutes for activity (at home or in class)
10 minutes for discussion

Classroom Organization

Individuals, followed by whole-class discussion

Doing the Activity

Be sure students have the formulas for the mean and standard deviation for the binomial distribution (from *The Search Is On!*) available.

Discussing and Debriefing the Activity

Question 1

Ask for volunteers to present Questions 1a and 1b. Students need to realize that these problems involve one-tail situations rather than symmetric intervals around the mean.

For instance, for Question 1a, the formulas from *The Search Is On!* give $\mu = 300 \cdot .53$, which is 159, and $\sigma = \sqrt{300 \cdot .53 \cdot .47}$, which is approximately 8.64. (*Note:* Save the value of σ for use in the discussion of *Is Twice as Many Twice as Good?*)

For the poll to show Coretta leading, she needs to get more than 150 votes. Here, as in other examples, there is a difficulty in using a continuous distribution to model a discrete situation. We will work with an interval that extends 9 votes below the mean. However, some students might say she needs at least 151 votes, so the interval should extend only 8 votes below the mean.

A margin of 9 votes is roughly 1.04 standard deviations (that is, $\dfrac{9}{8.64} \approx 1.04$), so students need to find the probability of being no more than 1.04σ below μ. Using linear interpolation with the table from *The Normal Table* gives a probability corresponding to $z = 1.04$ of approximately .7011, so approximately 70% of all results are within 1.04σ of μ. Half of the remaining 30% are more than 1.04σ above μ, so approximately 85% of all polls should show Coretta winning.

A similar analysis for Question 1b gives $\mu = 318$, $\sigma = \sqrt{600 \cdot .53 \cdot .47}$ (which is approximately 12.23), and a probability of approximately .93 that Coretta will come out ahead. (*Note:* Save the value of σ for use in the discussion of *Is Twice as Many Twice as Good?*)

Question 2: Why Does σ Go Up?

Discuss Question 2 as a whole class. You may need to clarify why there is a problem—that is, why one might expect σ to go down as n increases. Why might you expect the standard deviation to go down as the sample size gets bigger? Emphasize that bigger polls should give more accurate results. One might expect increased accuracy to be associated with a smaller standard deviation.

The answer involves the distinction between the *number* of votes and the *proportion* of votes. For instance, doubling the poll size from Question 1a to Question 2a did not double the standard deviation, but only increased it from approximately 8.6 to approximately 12.2. The standard deviation is a smaller fraction of the total number of votes for the larger poll than it is for the smaller poll. In the next activity, *From Numbers to Proportions,* students will see that if they study the distribution of the proportion of votes, the standard deviation does go down as the poll size increases.

Multiplying n by some factor multiplies the standard deviation by the square root of that factor. If students bring this up here, fine; otherwise, it will be brought out in the discussion of *Is Twice as Many Twice as Good?*

Key Question

Why might you expect the standard deviation to go down as the sample size gets bigger?

From Numbers to Proportions

Intent

Students develop formulas for the mean and standard deviation of the proportion of votes for a candidate in a poll.

Mathematics

Students now adapt their formulas for the mean and standard deviation in a polling situation to the proportion of votes instead of the number of votes.

Progression

Students find the formulas for mean and standard deviation of the proportion of votes for a candidate in a poll. The follow-up discussion helps them to transform their equation for standard deviation into a more commonly used form.

Approximate Time

40 minutes

Classroom Organization

Individuals or small groups, followed by whole-class discussion

Doing the Activity

Use the discussion of Question 2 of *Putting Your Formulas to Work* to motivate the need to find formulas like those in *The Search Is On!* for the distribution of sample proportions that come from a poll. In this activity, students will adjust the formulas for the mean and standard deviation from the situation of the *number of votes* to the situation of the *proportion of votes*.

You may want to clarify what is expected in Question 2a. For instance, if a candidate gets 285 votes out of 500, the candidate's *proportion* of votes is $\frac{285}{500}$. Students might leave this as a fraction, or they may prefer to express it as the decimal .57.

Note: If students enter their made-up poll results into their calculators, they can let the calculators find the mean and standard deviation. They can then convert the numbers in the list to proportions (perhaps expressed as decimals) and get the mean and standard deviation of the proportions.

Discussing and Debriefing the Activity

Students should see that their results for Question 2b are each exactly $\frac{1}{500}$ times the corresponding results for Question 1b.

Ask, **How do the computations show that this result makes sense?** You may want to focus on the computation for the mean, which is much simpler.

For instance, suppose the numbers in Question 1a are 265, 273, 241, 248, 285, and 230. The mean is found by the expression

$$\frac{265 + 273 + 241 + 248 + 285 + 230}{6}$$

The proportions for Question 2a are found by dividing each of the numbers 265, 273, 241, 248, 285, and 230 by 500, so the mean in Question 2b is given by the expression

$$\frac{\frac{265}{500} + \frac{273}{500} + \frac{241}{500} + \frac{248}{500} + \frac{285}{500} + \frac{230}{500}}{6}$$

Students should see that this expression is exactly $\frac{1}{500}$ times the expression for Question 1b. (This may be less obvious if students expressed the proportions as decimals or simplified the fractions.)

For the standard deviation, the reasoning is similar but messier. Use your judgment about whether to work through an example in detail.

Question 4: Adjusting the General Formulas

Let volunteers report their formulas for the mean and standard deviation of the proportion of votes the candidate gets in an *n*-person poll.

Students should have seen in Questions 1 to 3 that for a 500-person poll, the proportion of votes is $\frac{1}{500}$ times the number of votes and that the mean and standard deviation are also $\frac{1}{500}$ times as big. They should be able to generalize that for *n*-person polls, the mean and standard deviation for proportion of votes is $\frac{1}{n}$ times the mean and standard deviation for number of votes.

Students should then combine this principle with the formulas $\mu = np$ and $\sigma = \sqrt{np(1-p)}$ for the mean and standard deviation, respectively, of the *number* of votes. For clarity, you might label those values μ_{num} and σ_{num} to emphasize that they refer to the *number* of votes, and introduce the symbols μ_{prop} and σ_{prop} for the mean and standard deviation for the *proportion* of votes. (*Note:* Once the formulas for μ_{prop} and σ_{prop} have been established, there will be little need to use μ_{num} and σ_{num}, so after today's activity, this guide will represent μ_{prop} and σ_{prop} simply as μ and σ, without subscripts.)

Students' work should lead them to the principle that for the *proportion* of votes, the formula for the mean is

$$\mu_{prop} = \frac{\mu_{num}}{n} = \frac{np}{n} = p$$

Emphasize again that this is the "obvious" answer. That is, the average of all possible sample proportions should be the true proportion (the proportion in the overall population).

Similarly, for the proportion of votes, the formula for the standard deviation is

$$\sigma_{prop} = \frac{\sigma_{num}}{n} = \frac{\sqrt{np(1-p)}}{n}$$

Although this formula is correct as it stands, you might have students transform it into the more common form, $\sqrt{\dfrac{p(1-p)}{n}}$. If necessary, suggest writing the denominator as $\sqrt{n^2}$. Students can then simplify the expression as

$$\sigma_{prop} = \frac{\sqrt{np(1-p)}}{\sqrt{n^2}} = \sqrt{\frac{np(1-p)}{n^2}} = \sqrt{\frac{p(1-p)}{n}}$$

The formula $\sigma_{prop} = \sqrt{\dfrac{p(1-p)}{n}}$ shows that for proportions, σ goes down as n goes up. This fits what students should have seen in the earlier discussion of Question 2 of *Putting Your Formulas to Work*.

Summarize and post these "proportion versions" of the formulas for mean and standard deviation:

For the binomial distribution with n trials and probability p of success for each trial, the mean and the standard deviation for the *proportion* of successes are given by these formulas:

$$\mu_{prop} = p$$

$$\sigma_{prop} = \sqrt{\frac{p(1-p)}{n}}$$

Again, post a statement about how these formulas apply to polling:

If polls of size n are done in a population for which the true proportion is p (using sampling with replacement), then the mean and standard deviation for the proportion of "yes" votes are p and $\sqrt{\frac{p(1-p)}{n}}$, respectively.

That is, under the assumptions of this unit, these formulas give the mean and the standard deviation for the sample proportion.

Key Question

How do the computations show that this result makes sense?

Is Twice as Many Twice as Good?

Intent

Students see the effect of poll size on the standard deviation of poll results.

Mathematics

Students use their new formula to examine numerically how standard deviation varies with poll size.

Progression

Students compare the interval around the true proportion that has a 95% chance of containing their poll result for polls of two sizes, 200 and 400. They see that doubling the poll size divides σ not by 2, but by $\sqrt{2}$.

Approximate Time

25 minutes for activity (at home or in class)
10 minutes for discussion

Classroom Organization

Individuals, followed by whole-class discussion

Doing the Activity

Little or no introduction is required.

Discussing and Debriefing the Activity

You may want to have the presenter for Question 1 review the general formula

$\sigma = \sqrt{\dfrac{p(1-p)}{n}}$ for the standard deviation of the sample proportion.

Students should see that in this situation, $\sigma = \sqrt{\dfrac{.6 \cdot .4}{200}} \approx .035$ (because $p = .6$ and $n = 200$). This means that $2\sigma \approx .07$, so in the long run, 95% of the sample proportions will be between .53 (which is $\mu - 2\sigma$) and .67 (which is $\mu + 2\sigma$). In other words, in any particular 200-person poll, there is a 95% chance that the poll will show the candidate getting between 53% and 67% of the vote.

The purpose of Question 2 is to see how a change in n affects σ. Be sure students see that doubling n (from 200 to 400) does *not* make σ half as big. The formula gives $\sigma = \sqrt{\dfrac{.6 \cdot .4}{400}} \approx .0245$.

Emphasize that this new standard deviation is *not* half the value of σ from Question 1. Then ask, **What size poll *would* be needed to make the value of σ half what it is in Question 1 (and to make the interval containing 95% of the poll results half as big as well)?**

Students may look for this value of n purely numerically. That is, they may look for a value of n that makes $\sqrt{\dfrac{.6 \cdot .4}{n}}$ equal to approximately half of the value they got for σ in Question 1. With this approach, their answer will depend on the approximate value they found for that value of σ. If they use $\sigma = .035$, they will be solving the equation $\sqrt{\dfrac{.6 \cdot .4}{n}} = \dfrac{.035}{2}$, which gives roughly $n = 784$.

Others may look at the formula for σ ($\sigma = \sqrt{\dfrac{p(1 - p)}{n}}$), see that σ is inversely proportional to the square root of n, and reason that one would need to quadruple n to halve σ.

If students use only a numeric approach at first, insist they get a more accurate value for n than 784. (They need to use four significant digits for the standard deviation—that is, $\sigma = .03464$—to get $n \approx 800$. Or, solve the equation using the exact value of σ, $\sqrt{\dfrac{.6 \cdot .4}{n}} = \dfrac{1}{2}\sqrt{\dfrac{.6 \cdot .4}{200}}$.) Once they see that n should be 800, point out that this is four times the original value of n—that is, halving σ requires quadrupling n. Then go over how this fact can be derived algebraically from the general formula.

Another Example

You can get another example of the connection between changes in n and changes in σ using the results from *Putting Your Formulas to Work* (even though these results involve *numbers* of votes instead of *proportions*). Review those results, bringing out that in going from a 300- to a 600-person poll, the standard deviation increases from approximately 8.64 to approximately 12.23.

Ask students, **By what factor does σ go up when we double the poll size?** They can divide 12.23 by 8.64 to see that σ increases by a factor of approximately

1.416. The important thing is to identify this factor as approximately $\sqrt{2}$. (The "approximately" is needed, because the two values for σ are rounded off.)

Key Questions

What size poll *would* be needed to make the value of σ half what it is in Question 1 (and to make the interval containing 95% of the poll results half as big as well)?
By what factor does σ go up when we double the poll size?

A Matter of Confidence

Intent

In these activities, students see how the confidence they can have in a poll's result can be measured mathematically.

Mathematics

These activities introduce students to the concepts of confidence level, confidence interval, and margin of error. Students see how these concepts are interrelated and related to sample size and, surprisingly, how they are relatively independent of population size. Students begin to plan a polling project that they will complete with a partner.

Progression

Different p, Different σ introduces the concept of confidence intervals. Students see that because the sample size, true proportion, and standard deviation of a theoretical polling distribution are all mutually dependent, it is necessary to make an assumption about the true proportion in order to select a sample size that will yield the desired margin of error. They arrive at the most commonly used (and most conservative) assumed value for the true proportion in *The Worst-Case Scenario*. Students further explore the relationships between sample size, margin of error, and confidence level in *What Does It Mean?*, *Confidence and Sample Size*, and *Polling Puzzles*.

Let's Vote on It! introduces a polling project that will span much of the remainder of the unit. Students make initial plans for their poll in *Project Topics and Random Polls*. They finalize those plans in *How Big?* once they understand how to select an appropriate sample size.

Different p, Different σ
Let's Vote on It!
Project Topics and Random Polls
Mean, Median, and Mode
The Worst-Case Scenario
A Teaching Dilemma
What Does It Mean?
Confidence and Sample Size
Polling Puzzles
How Big?

Different p, Different σ

Intent

This activity introduces confidence intervals and gives students more experience working with the formula for σ.

Mathematics

Students learn to establish a confidence interval in terms of a sample proportion and the standard deviation. They then begin to examine how σ and the confidence interval depend on the true proportion. In the process, they explore the dilemma that one cannot establish a confidence interval without already knowing the value of p.

Progression

The activity opens with a class discussion about how to estimate the true proportion. Students summarize what they know and are reminded that the sample proportion is probably the best guess for the true proportion. The discussion clarifies that the remaining issue is the level of confidence about the estimate for the true proportion. The teacher then defines the terms *95% confidence interval* and *confidence level*. Then, given the sample size and sample proportion for a poll, students determine three things for two different true proportions: the value of σ, the endpoints of the 95% confidence interval around the sample proportion, and whether p is within the confidence interval.

Approximate Time

30 to 40 minutes

Classroom Organization

Whole-class discussion, followed by individuals or small groups and further whole-class discussion

Materials

Optional: Transparencies of *Different p, Different σ* blackline masters

Doing the Activity

Introduce the topic by asking, What is the purpose of doing an election poll? Help students to articulate that pollsters take election polls to find the true proportion—that is, to determine the fraction of voters in the overall population supporting a certain candidate.

Remind students that in *Is Twice as Many Twice as Good?*, and in much of the unit so far, they have been working backward: assuming they know the true proportion and studying what happens when a pollster takes a poll from that population. Now they will turn the process around.

Summarizing the Known Results

Review with students what they know about this question: What happens when a pollster takes a poll from a population with true proportion p? They should be able to summarize the results like this:

> **If the true proportion is p and the poll size is n, then the distribution of sample proportions is approximately normal, and the approximating normal distribution has mean p and standard deviation $\sqrt{\dfrac{p(1-p)}{n}}$.**

Review the specific case of Question 1 of *Is Twice as Many Twice as Good?*, with $p = .6$ and $n = 200$, for which $\mu = .6$ and $\sigma \approx .035$. For emphasis, go over the principle that 95% of the results are within two standard deviations of the mean—that is, between $\mu - 2\sigma$ and $\mu + 2\sigma$. In this case, this means that 95% of 200-person polls will give values of $\hat{p}$ between .53 and .67.

You might want to ask students to draw a picture of what's happening using a number line. The diagram here (which is included on a blackline master) indicates that for 95% of all 200-person polls with $p = .6$, $\hat{p}$ will be in the shaded area, which extends 2σ in either direction from p.

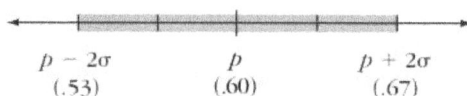

$p - 2\sigma$	p	$p + 2\sigma$
(.53)	(.60)	(.67)

Summarize this example with a statement like this and then post it:

> **Approximately 95% of all sample proportions are within 2σ of the true proportion.**

Emphasize that this is true no matter what the value of p is. (*Note:* This statement is not specifically about polling, but rather is simply a fact about normal distributions.)

Review Assumptions About n

Ask, *What assumptions underlie the use of the normal distribution to analyze poll results?* Students should articulate two key assumptions:

- The population must be much larger than the poll size so that the poll can be accurately modeled using sampling with replacement.
- The poll size must be large enough that the normal distribution is a good approximation for the binomial distribution.

The rules of thumb mentioned previously (see the discussions of *Bags of Marbles and Bowls of Ice Cream* and *The Theory of Polls*) state that these assumptions hold as long as n is at most 5% of the population and np and $n(1 - p)$ are both at least 5. In the case of the opening unit problem, the overall population is 400,000, so the first assumption holds as long as n is at most 20,000. If p is anywhere between .2 and .8, the second assumption holds as long as n is at least 25. The poll size of the opening problem—500—fits both conditions.

The Best Guess for p

With this summary of what they know about poll results if they have the value of p, students are ready to look at how to find p if all they know is the result of one poll.

Tell students to imagine that they have taken one poll, of size n, and ask, *If you got $\hat{p}$ for your sample proportion, what would you guess for p?* Students will probably suggest the obvious guess: using $\hat{p}$ itself for p. Assure them that this is, indeed, the best possible guess.

In fact, the distribution for $\hat{p}$ has mean p, which confirms that the expected value for $\hat{p}$ is exactly p. In other words, over many polls, the values of $\hat{p}$ average out to p. This is similar to the fact that as one tosses a fair coin many times, the proportion of heads gets closer and closer to 50%.

The Question of Confidence

Tell the class that the key remaining question is this:

> **If you use $\hat{p}$ as your guess for the value of p, how confident should you be about this guess?**

More specifically, students need to determine how likely it is that their guess will differ from the real value of p by any given amount.

Point out that they have seen that 95% of the time, the value of $\hat{p}$ is within 2σ of p. The goal of the next part of the discussion is to bring out the "obvious" statement that if $\hat{p}$ is within 2σ of p, then p is within 2σ of $\hat{p}$.

Starting from $\hat{p}$

Now ask students to imagine that they know only $\hat{p}$ and want to draw a conclusion about p. Again, using the situation from Question 1 of *Is Twice as Many Twice as Good?*, give students a specific value for $\hat{p}$ in the interval from $\mu - 2\sigma$ to $\mu + 2\sigma$ (that is, from .53 to .67) and have them discuss how far p might be from $\hat{p}$. As needed, point to the posted statement:

> **Approximately 95% of all sample proportions are within 2σ of the true proportion.**

To illustrate, you might tell students to suppose they did a poll and got $\hat{p} = .581$, and ask, If $\hat{p} = .581$, what does that tell you about p?

Students will likely say there's a 95% chance that p will be within two standard deviations of $\hat{p}$. They may point out that they need to know what σ is to find this interval numerically. If so, tell them that for now, they can express their answer in terms of σ. (If they are uncomfortable with this, have them use the value of .035 found earlier. They will examine this issue in today's activity and in *The Worst-Case Scenario*.)

Students can illustrate the situation with a diagram like this one (which is also on a blackline master). We expect to find p somewhere in the shaded interval. (*Note:* If students use .035 for σ, they would give the values .511 and .651 for the endpoints of the shaded interval.)

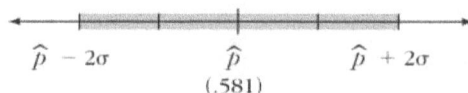

$$\hat{p} - 2\sigma \qquad \hat{p} \atop (.581) \qquad \hat{p} + 2\sigma$$

Tell students that this interval around $\hat{p}$ is called a 95% **confidence interval,** because 95% of the time, the value of p is within 2σ of $\hat{p}$. (The distinction between *probability* and *confidence* will be discussed in the introduction to *The Worst-Case Scenario*.)

Point out that although the interval of width 2σ is the one most commonly used, there is nothing magical about 95%. For instance, we could use the term "68% confidence interval" for an interval of width σ around $\hat{p}$. The percentage associated with the interval is called the *confidence level*. (In fact, one can ask about the confidence level for any interval, even one not symmetric about the mean. This will come up in *What Does It Mean?*)

If students haven't yet raised the issue, point out that in order to describe precisely the interval within two standard deviations of $\hat{p}$, they need to know the value of σ. But the formula for σ is expressed in terms of p, and the whole purpose of the poll is to find p! There's something circular about giving a confidence interval for p whose size itself depends on p.

In this activity, students will examine the relationship between σ and p in connection with the idea of a 95% confidence interval.

Discussing and Debriefing the Activity

Let volunteers present the various questions. Be sure students see that the confidence interval is centered around $\hat{p}$, not around p.

- Question 1: $\sigma \approx .111$, the 95% confidence interval is from .378 to .822, and p is within the confidence interval.
- Question 2: $\sigma \approx .089$, the 95% confidence interval is from .421 to .779, and p is outside the confidence interval.

Bring out that although p changes substantially, from .55 to .80, the value of σ does not change nearly as much.

Key Questions

What is the purpose of doing an election poll?
What happens when a pollster takes a poll from a population with true proportion p?
What does this look like on the number line?
What assumptions underlie the use of the normal distribution to analyze poll results?
If you got $\hat{p}$ for your sample proportion, what would you guess for p?
If $\hat{p} = .581$, what does that tell you about p?

Let's Vote on It!

Intent

Students undertake a polling project in which they apply the concepts from the entire unit.

Mathematics

In this project, students apply what they have learned about designing a poll, identifying a population to be polled, determining the sample size that will yield a desired level of confidence, selecting a random population sample, and evaluating the polling results.

Progression

In this project activity, students work with a partner to design and conduct a poll about a topic and population of their choice. In *Project Topics and Random Polls*, they propose topics and populations and begin to think about how they will design the poll. In *How Big?*, they select a confidence level and sample size and then submit their refined plans for the project. Partners then collect data over a two- to three-day interval, complete their data analysis, submit a written report, and present a brief oral report.

Approximate Time

10 minutes for introduction
2 to 3 hours for activity, plus additional class time as noted under "Project Stages and Timeline" in the discussion notes below

Classroom Organization

Teacher presentation today, followed by partners working in and out of class over a period of a week or more

Doing the Activity

Tell students that the culmination of this unit is a polling project that they will do in pairs. Take a minute or two right now to have students choose partners.

In this activity, *Let's Vote on It*, students will do individual write-ups. They will make tentative decisions about a topic for their poll, about an overall population from which to take their sample, and about procedures for choosing the sample and providing anonymity to participants. Through the follow-up discussion, they will get clearer ideas about these aspects of their projects and will be ready to begin working with their partners.

Review the main aspects of the project:

- A poll topic must have two sides or a two-way preference and should concern a subject about which people are unlikely to be undecided. (Use the later discussion of *Project Topics and Random Polls* to verify that topics are mathematically and socially appropriate.)
- The overall population should be one for which students can obtain a reasonably random sample. "American adults" is not a good choice, because students have no way of getting a random sample from this group. "Adults who shop at a certain mall between certain hours" is a more feasible population to work with.
- Students need to specify a clear procedure for conducting a random sample of their population so they don't simply end up asking people they feel most comfortable with or most curious about. Picking people by "whim" is not random.
- According to the guidelines for sampling with replacement, the poll size should be at most 5% of the overall population. If your school is small, this may mean students have to go outside the school to obtain a sufficiently large overall population. Students will learn more about the poll size they need in the next few activities.
- Students need to think about how to give people enough privacy while they are voting so that the poll has a better chance of getting honest returns.

Project Stages and Timeline

Here is a summary of the stages of this project:

- Students are introduced to *Let's Vote on It!* and choose partners.
- In *Project Topics and Random Polls,* students pick tentative topics and overall populations, and they think about sampling and polling issues. Through the subsequent discussion, they refine their ideas about polling procedures.
- In *How Big?,* Students decide on a confidence level and confidence interval, determine the necessary sample size, and turn in their topics and plans.
- Students collect their project data over a two- to three-day period. Completing this data collection is their task in *Final Data Collection*.
- Students work in class on their projects for at least 40 to 60 minutes, analyzing their data and preparing their oral presentations.
- Students turn in their written reports and present their 5-minute oral reports. As time allows, other students pose questions to the presenters about their methodology and their conclusions.

Project Topics and Random Polls

Intent

Students begin to plan their polling projects.

Mathematics

This activity involves the concepts of identifying a population, selecting a random sample, and the importance of anonymity in polling situations.

Progression

Partners choose a tentative topic for their project and formulate their polling question. In addition, they select the population for their poll, decide how they will choose a random sample, and decide how they will provide participants with anonymity. They will select their sample size later, in *How Big?*

Subsequently, partners are given time to confer. A whole-class discussion then centers around evaluating the proposals, which are briefly presented by each pair of students. All of the decisions made by individual students in preparing the written assignment may be revised as partners have an opportunity to come to agreement and participate in subsequent discussions.

Approximate Time

30 minutes for activity (at home or in class)
40 minutes for discussion

Classroom Organization

Individuals, followed by discussion between partners and then whole-class discussion

Doing the Activity

No introduction to this activity is needed.

Discussing and Debriefing the Activity

The goal of this discussion is to help students clarify their project topics, populations, and methods of data collection. Before starting the discussion, allow time for partners to share their ideas with each other and agree on a topic.

Then begin a class discussion about topics and overall populations, allowing each pair of students to share their tentative decisions. You and other students might comment on the appropriateness and feasibility of each idea.

For instance, help students to phrase their polling questions in simple yes-or-no form and to avoid questions that are likely to lead to many undecided participants. Also help them to define their overall population clearly. That is, ensure the appropriateness of the population for the polling question and eliminate any ambiguity as to who belongs to the population.

Then turn to the polling procedures students plan to use, again giving each pair of students an opportunity to share their ideas. Much of the discussion will likely focus on how to achieve (or at least closely approximate) randomness. You may need to take the lead in pointing out flaws in students' methods and suggesting alternatives.

For example, if students use "all students in the school" as their overall population and plan to choose participants by stopping people as they leave school, you might point out that some students stay later at school to participate in special activities or that students leave school by different exits.

Finally, discuss the issue of how to assure participants that their individual answers cannot be identified. For instance, if participants are marking a box on a slip of paper, have students clarify exactly how they will handle those slips of paper. Will the papers be put into a sealed box? Or will they simply be handed to the person conducting the poll? Point out that the degree of anonymity required may vary with the sensitivity of the topic. For instance, participants might be less concerned about privacy if the question concerns a choice between plaids and stripes than if it concerns something of a more personal nature.

Mean, Median, and Mode

Intent

Students review the meanings and uses of the terms *mean, median,* and *mode.*

Mathematics

Students deepen their understanding of the three basic measures of central tendency.

Progression

Students define *mean, median,* and *mode;* calculate each measure for a given set of data; and then make up situations in which each of the three would be the most meaningful measure of central tendency.

Approximate Time

30 minutes for activity (at home or in class)
10 minutes for discussion

Classroom Organization

Individuals, followed by whole-class discussion

Doing the Activity

No introduction to this activity is needed.

Discussing and Debriefing the Activity

Begin by having volunteers state the definition of each of the three terms and illustrate the meaning using a simple data set, such as 3, 5, 6, 7, 8, 8, 10, and 11. Clarify as needed that a data set may have more than one mode and that if it has an even number of elements, the median might not be one of them.

Then turn to the example in Question 2. Students probably found it helpful to explicitly list the data items, showing each outcome with the appropriate frequency:

0, 0, 0, 1, 2, 2, 2, 2, 2, 3, 3, 3, 4, 4, 4, 4, 4, 4, 5, 5, 5, 5, 5, 5, 5, 5, 6, 6, 6, 6

They should see that there are 30 items in the list and that their sum is

$$(3 \cdot 0) + (1 \cdot 1) + (5 \cdot 2) + (3 \cdot 3) + (6 \cdot 4) + (8 \cdot 5) + (4 \cdot 6)$$

The mean is thus $108 \div 30$, which students might write as $3\frac{3}{5}$ or 3.6.

Students should also explain that because the fifteenth and sixteenth terms are both equal to 4, this value is the median. Finally, they should point out that because the outcome 5 occurs more often than any other, it is the mode.

No specific conclusions need to come out of Question 2b. If students make statements about the median such as "the student gets scores above the median as often as scores below it," caution them that this won't always be the case. For instance, if there were two more scores of 6 in the data set, the median would still be 4, but there would be more scores above 4 than below 4.

You might also point out that although 5 is the most common score, the student is more likely to get a score *different* from 5 than to get that particular score.

For Question 3, ask volunteers to share a couple of examples for each measure of central tendency. Have the class discuss the "usefulness" of each measure in the situations described.

The Worst-Case Scenario

Intent

Students learn how to determine a standard deviation for a poll that will lead to the desired confidence interval.

Mathematics

Students have previously considered the dilemma that the standard deviation for their poll is dependent upon the true proportion, which is not known or there would be no need for a poll. Strategies for dealing with this are now discussed, including the conservative approach of planning for the worst-case scenario. Students see that σ is maximized when the population is evenly divided. They also discuss the terms *margin of error, confidence,* and *probability*.

Progression

The teacher first has students consider a typical news use of the term *margin of error,* including the ideas that it usually refers to a 95% confidence interval and that "confidence" is not the same as "probability." The class then shares ideas on what to use for σ and discusses both the "estimation approach" and the "conservative approach." Students then determine the value of p that gives the largest value of σ, for multiple values of n. The subsequent discussion confirms that for any value of n, σ has its maximum value when $p = .5$. Students then prove this.

Approximate Time

40 minutes

Classroom Organization

Whole-class discussion, followed by small groups, then further whole-class discussion

Materials

Optional: A news article using the phrase *margin of error*

Doing the Activity

Note: If possible, replace the fictitious example used here with one from an actual news article.

Read or post the following fictitious statement, and ask students what they think it means, particularly in terms of the phrase *margin of error*:

> **"Our poll shows that 57% of the voters plan to vote for Shirley Shoe-in. The margin of error for this poll is plus or minus 4 percentage points."**

Let two or three volunteers share their ideas. They should mention that the statement gives the impression that the percentage of voters planning to vote for Shirley Shoe-in *must be* between 53% and 61%.

Tell students that the phrase *margin of error* refers to the "radius" of a confidence interval—that is, the distance the interval extends in either direction from the mean. In common usage, the confidence level is 95%, so the margin of error is usually two standard deviations.

Remind students that there are other confidence intervals besides the interval of width 2σ, and mention that the popular news media usually talk about a margin of error without giving the confidence level. When this term is used without mentioning a confidence level, readers should assume it refers to a 95% confidence level. (Perhaps news media omit mention of a confidence level because they don't get that information from pollsters. And perhaps pollsters omit it because they don't think the public will understand what a confidence level is.)

Confidence Versus Probability

The term *confidence level* is used instead of *probability* because probability generally refers to a future situation, not a fixed but unknown past or current situation.

On the one hand, if we have a poll result (a sample proportion) of 53% in favor of our candidate, it doesn't exactly make sense to talk about the *probability* that the true proportion is within 2σ of our result. Either it is or it isn't.

On the other hand, *before we take the poll,* we can say there is a probability of .95 that the sample proportion $\hat{p}$ will be within 2σ of the true proportion. Saying that $\hat{p}$ is within 2σ of p is, of course, the same as saying that p is within 2σ of $\hat{p}$. But the point here is that $\hat{p}$ is the "variable," not p.

Nevertheless, for 95% of our polls, the true proportion will end up within 2σ of our sample proportion. Mathematicians express this by saying that we have 95% *confidence* that the true proportion is within 2σ of the sample proportion.

How Do You Choose σ?

As needed, review the ideas of a *confidence interval* and a *confidence level,* perhaps focusing on the case of a 95% confidence interval. Help students see that in a given situation, roughly 95% of all polls will give a sample percentage $\hat{p}$ that is within two standard deviations of the true percentage p. If you have taken a sample and gotten $\hat{p}$, you can be "95% confident" that p is within two standard deviations of this value. That is, p should lie somewhere between $\hat{p} - 2\sigma$ and $\hat{p} + 2\sigma$.

Then point out that the formula for σ itself depends on the value of p. And when you take a poll, you don't know p, creating a dilemma for determining a correct confidence interval.

Ask students how they think this "dilemma of σ"—that is, the issue that they can't calculate σ if they don't know p—should be resolved. **What should you do about σ if you don't know p?**

At least two ideas should be mentioned, which we might call the "estimation approach" and the "conservative approach." If students don't suggest both, bring them up yourself.

The estimation approach: Calculate σ using $\hat{p}$ as an estimate for p. In other words, use $\sqrt{\dfrac{\hat{p}(1 - \hat{p})}{n}}$ as an estimate for σ. This approach, although reasonable, has some difficulties. Here are two issues to bring up:
- With this approach, you can't determine the margin of error until after you've done your poll.
- If your estimate for σ is smaller than the correct value, you get a confidence level that is too large.

The conservative approach: The conservative approach—which most pollsters follow—is to use the largest value σ could possibly have. In other words, pollsters take into account the worst possible case. That way, they know there is *at least* a 95% chance that the true proportion will be in their confidence interval.

Before students begin working, you might want to go over why the activity is called *The Worst-Case Scenario*. In the activity, students figure out the largest value σ might have. The result is expressed in terms of the size of the poll.

Discussing and Debriefing the Activity

Let students from two or three groups discuss their results and methods. Here are some "experimental" approaches they may have used (see the next subsection for other, more algebraic, ideas):

- Using guess-and-check by plugging values of p into the expression $\sqrt{\dfrac{p(1 - p)}{500}}$

- Using a calculator to graph the function defined by the equation

$$f(p) = \sqrt{\frac{p(1-p)}{500}}$$

- Using a calculator to get a table for this function

Whichever approach students use, they should see that the maximum value of σ occurs when $p = .5$. Help them understand that this maximum value is $\sqrt{\frac{.5 \cdot .5}{n}}$, and have students simplify this to $\frac{.5}{\sqrt{n}}$. Then post this result:

For any value of n, the expression $\sqrt{\frac{p(1-p)}{n}}$ has its maximum when $p = .5$, and this maximum is $\frac{.5}{\sqrt{n}}$.

For the polling situation, having $p = .5$ means the population is evenly split between the two candidates. In other words, the closest elections make for the least reliable polls.

Why the Maximum Is Always at $p = .5$

If it has not yet been discussed, ask, Why does the maximum value for σ always occurs at $p = .5$? Students should see that for any n, the maximum for σ occurs when $p(1 - p)$ is a maximum, so this doesn't depend on n.

Students should be able to use their understanding of quadratic functions (perhaps by completing the square) to prove that the expression $p - p^2$ has its maximum at $p = .5$. For instance, they might write $p - p^2$ as $-(p - .5)^2 + .25$.

Variations in σ

Point out that although students just found the maximum value for σ, the fact is that σ doesn't change much unless p differs substantially from .5. For instance, if $p = .7$, then σ is $\sqrt{\frac{.7 \cdot .3}{n}}$, or approximately $\frac{.46}{\sqrt{n}}$, which is not much different from $\frac{.5}{\sqrt{n}}$.

Ask, What happens in the two extreme cases, $p = 0$ and $p = 1$? These special cases were considered in the discussion of *The Search Is On!*, but it's worth mentioning them again. Students should see that $\sigma = 0$ in both cases. Ask them to explain why this makes sense. They should note that in each case, the population is unanimous in its opinion, so there should be no variation among polls.

Key Questions

What should you do about σ if you don't know p?

Why does the maximum value for σ always occur at $p = .5$?

What happens in the two extreme cases, $p = 0$ and $p = 1$?

Supplemental Activity

***It's the News* (reinforcement)** asks students to find and comment on shortcomings in a news-media report of a poll.

A Teaching Dilemma

Intent

This activity, which is similar to *More Middletown Musings,* provides an opportunity for students to review the use of the normal table.

Mathematics

Students review the use of the normal distribution.

Progression

Students investigate data concerning the mean and standard deviation of a set of test scores.

Approximate Time

25 to 30 minutes for activity (at home or in class)
10 minutes for discussion

Classroom Organization

Individuals, followed by whole-class discussion

Doing the Activity

This activity requires no introduction.

Discussing and Debriefing the Activity

Note: We will discuss this problem as if the grading system were continuous. See the discussion notes for Question 2 of *More Middletown Musings* for an example of how to make adjustments if you assume the grades are whole numbers.

For Question 1, students should see that a grade of 85 would be roughly 2.2 standard deviations above the mean [because $(85 - 72) \div 5.9 \approx 2.2$]. *The Normal Table* shows that roughly 97% of all results are within two standard deviations of the mean, so approximately 3% are beyond this range. Of this 3%, half are on the "high" end, so approximately 1.5% of Ms. Gordon's students would earn A's. If she has five classes with 30 students each, then perhaps two of the 150 students would earn A's.

For Question 2, students should see that they need to find a *z*-value for which 6% (that is, twice 3%) of the results are beyond *z* standard deviations. *The Normal Table* shows that *z* is just under 1.9. (Linear interpolation gives $z \approx 1.882$.) An interval of 1.9 standard deviations represents $1.9 \cdot 5.9 \approx 11.2$ points on the grading scale. That is, scores above 83.2 would be more than 1.9 standard deviations above the mean. Therefore, if Ms. Gordon gives A's to students with scores above 83, roughly 3% of them will earn A's. In this case, out of 150 students, she would likely give four or five A's.

The simplest way to answer Question 3 is to choose an interval centered around the mean. If the interval contains 80% of all results, this corresponds to a *z*-value of approximately 1.3—that is, to the set of values within 1.3 standard deviations of the mean. This represents $1.3 \cdot 5.9 \approx 7.7$ points on the grading scale, so this would mean giving C's to students with scores from 64.3 to 79.7.

There are other possible answers to Question 3, though. For instance, suppose Ms. Gordon decided to give C's to the bottom 80% of her class. This group can be thought of as combining the middle 60% with the bottom 20%. The z-value corresponding to the middle 60% is approximately 0.8, which corresponds to roughly 4.7 points on the scoring scale. Thus, the C range would include all scores up to approximately 76.7. (Notice that the first solution—scores from 64.3 to 79.7— is a much "smaller" interval than the second—scores from 0 to 76.7. This means there would be about as many scores between 76.7 and 79.7 as below 64.3.)

What Does It Mean?

Intent

Students examine how to find the sample size in terms of the desired margin of error.

Mathematics

In practice, pollsters typically determine the margin of error they would like to have and use the worst-case scenario for σ to determine the sample size that will be needed. In this activity, students work with the concept of confidence interval and determine the sample size that was used to get the stated margin of error for a given poll.

Progression

Students estimate the size of a poll based on its reported margin of error. The subsequent discussion reviews that margin of error usually refers to a 95% confidence interval. It also goes over the algebra of estimating the sample size.

Approximate Time

40 minutes

Classroom Organization

Small groups or individuals, followed by whole-class discussion

Doing the Activity

No introduction to this activity is needed.

Discussing and Debriefing the Activity

Students may want to discuss the issue of whether a random telephone poll of registered voters reaches the group whose opinion really matters, as it certainly will not include the homeless themselves. (Some of them might be registered voters, but they won't be easily reachable by telephone.) Use your judgment about how much time to spend on this and other issues beyond the mathematics of the problem.

The Politics of Formulating Questions

You might begin by mentioning that the results of a poll like this can be heavily influenced by how the question is posed. For example, here are two possible formulations:

> Because no better facilities seem to be available, which of these options do you favor?
> (a) Letting homeless people sleep in City Hall
> (b) Having homeless people sleep in the streets

> River City is thinking of letting homeless people sleep in City Hall overnight. Do you favor this proposal?

Ask students, *How do you think the results would compare if separate surveys were done using each of these two methods?* They will probably agree that people would be more likely to support the proposal if the pollster used the first formulation, because it presents respondents with a stark choice. With the second formulation, respondents don't need to consider what will happen to the homeless if the proposal is rejected.

Question 1

Let a volunteer explain how to find the confidence interval. In this case, the sample proportion is 52% and the margin of error is plus or minus 4%, so the confidence interval is from 48% to 56%.

Question 2

Ask a couple of students to explain their answers to Question 2. The "standard" interpretation is that the interval from .48 to .56 is a 95% confidence interval. That is, one can have 95% confidence that the true proportion is between .48 and .56.

You might remind students that when they read or hear statements about margin of error in the media, they generally can assume the statements are using a 95% confidence level.

Question 3

The key idea in Question 3 is that the margin of error represents an interval of length 2σ, so students need to use the equation $2\sigma = .04$ to find the value of n.

To find n, they should express σ in terms of n, the formula $\sigma = \sqrt{\dfrac{p(1-p)}{n}}$. They might use .52 as an estimate for p, or they might use the worst-case value, $p = .5$.

These two approaches give virtually the same result: $p = .5$ gives $\sigma = \dfrac{.5}{\sqrt{n}}$ while

$p = .52$ gives $\sigma \approx \dfrac{.4996}{\sqrt{n}}$.

The arithmetic is simpler using $p = .5$, and the equation $2\sigma = .04$ becomes

$$2 \cdot \frac{.5}{\sqrt{n}} = .04$$

Students will probably simplify this to $\dfrac{1}{\sqrt{n}} = .04$, which gives $n = 625$.

Bring out that in reporting the margin of error, the polling group or news source may have rounded off the value, so the actual value of n might be different. You might have students investigate this question: What range of values for n would give a margin of error that rounds off to 4% (that is, a margin of error between 3.5% and 4.5%)? It turns out that the value of n can range from 494 to 816.

You may want to review once again the key assumptions involved in using the normal distribution as a model for the distribution of polling results:

- n is "small enough" (less than 5% of the overall population), so sampling with replacement is an appropriate model
- n is "big enough" [both np and $n(1 - p)$ are at least 5], so the binomial distribution is approximately normal

The second condition is certainly true here, with n at least several hundred and p quite close to .5. Using $n = 625$, the first condition means that the overall population should be at least 12,500.

Question 4

Question 4 asks how confident one can be that a majority of voters support the city's plan. Mention that this is an important question to ask of any survey like this. Assuming the survey is a random sample of voters, this means finding out the confidence level for the interval from .50 on up. You may need to point out that the term *confidence level* can be applied to any interval, not just to those symmetric about the mean.

Students should be able to explain that σ is .02 (because they used $2\sigma = .04$ earlier). Thus, the interval above .50 consists of all values no lower than one standard deviation below the sample proportion.

As with earlier one-tail problems, there are a couple of ways to get the corresponding confidence level. Using a diagram like the one shown here, students might get the value in two ways:

- As the interval from .50 to .52 (which is half the shaded area) plus the interval above .52 (which has area .5)
- As the interval above .54 (which is half the unshaded area) plus the shaded area

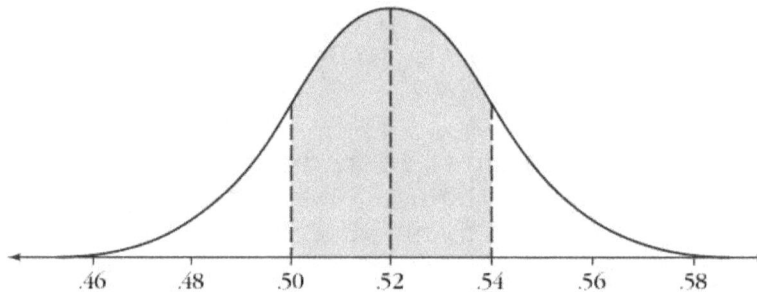

The Normal Table shows that the shaded area is .6827. The two approaches described here both yield a total area of roughly .84. That is, one can be 84% confident that a majority of the population supports the city's plan.

Key Questions

How do you think the results would compare if separate surveys were done using each of these two methods?
What range of values for *n* would give a margin of error that rounds off to 4% (that is, a margin of error between 3.5% and 4.5%)?

Confidence and Sample Size

Intent

Students consider the relationship between population size and sample size.

Mathematics

This activity raises the idea that with the assumption that sampling with replacement is a good model, the overall population size does not affect a poll's reliability.

Progression

After summarizing several key ideas in their own words, students examine the issue of when a poll is "big enough." The subsequent discussion clarifies that the accuracy of a poll depends on the size of the poll, but not on what fraction of the population that sample represents.

Approximate Time

30 minutes for activity (at home or in class)
10 minutes for discussion

Classroom Organization

Individuals, followed by whole-class discussion

Doing the Activity

This activity needs no introduction.

Discussing and Debriefing the Activity

Question 1

Have two or three volunteers share their ideas about the concepts of confidence interval, confidence level, and margin of error.

The next activity, *Polling Puzzles,* concerns the numeric relationships among confidence level, margin of error, and poll size. You may want to emphasize that a margin of error is essentially nothing more than another way to describe a confidence interval (at least for intervals symmetric about the mean). Thus, these two concepts are not independent of each other.

Question 2

Ask students to come to agreement in their groups about who is right, Jen or Ken. Although Ken is basically correct, many students may intuitively agree with Jen. Their feeling may persist even though they have just gone through the mathematical analysis that disproves it.

The key idea is that, *at least up to a point,* the poll's reliability does not depend on how big a fraction it represents of the overall population. Rather, it depends on the absolute size of the poll. Throughout this unit, we have been assuming that our sample sizes are less than 5% of the overall population, in order to use the model of sampling with replacement. As long as this assumption is valid, the size of the overall population does not matter. For instance, a 200-person poll from a 40,000-person population will be no more reliable than a 200-person poll from a 400,000-person population.

Acknowledge that if the sample size is a significant portion of an overall population, the poll will be more reliable than a poll of the same size from a much larger population. For instance, a 200-person poll from a 210-person population will be more reliable than a 200-person poll from a 400,000-person population. That is, if we drop the assumption that the sample size is much smaller than the overall population, Jen may actually be correct.

If you get students to recognize the role of the "sampling with replacement" model, that may help them see why their intuition leads them astray. You might point out that using sampling with replacement is essentially the same as assuming that the overall population is "infinitely large," so its exact size no longer matters.

Given the assumption that the overall population is very large, have students do the following:

- Imagine two large containers, each with marbles of two colors and each with the colors in the same proportion, such as one-third of one color and two-thirds of the other.
- Imagine that one container is a large barrel holding 10,000 marbles and the other is a huge vat holding 100,000 marbles. Assume the marbles in each container are thoroughly mixed.
- Imagine dipping a scoop into each container to get a large sample of marbles (perhaps 100 or 200).

Students may recognize that both scoops give a fairly reliable picture of the proportion in which the two colors of marbles appear in the containers.

You may also want to acknowledge that "true things" don't always feel intuitively correct. That is one reason for doing theoretical analyses.

Polling Puzzles

Intent

Students explore the connections among confidence level, margin of error, and sample size.

Mathematics

In this activity, students investigate the relationships among the concepts of confidence level, margin of error, and sample size.

Progression

In each of four questions, students are given two of the three variables of margin of error, confidence level, and sample size and are asked to find the third.

Approximate Time

25 to 30 minutes for activity (at home or in class)
5 to 10 minutes for discussion

Classroom Organization

Individuals or small groups, followed by whole-class discussion

Doing the Activity

You might choose some students to prepare presentations of their work.

Discussing and Debriefing the Activity

The questions are fairly straightforward applications of the formula relating σ to n and of *The Normal Table* relating probability (or confidence level) to the number of standard deviations in the interval. Because no sample proportions are available, students should use the worst-case scenario, which means using the formula

$$\sigma = \frac{.5}{\sqrt{n}}.$$

Have volunteers present each problem. In Question 1, the presenter might explain that *The Normal Table* tells us that the 95% confidence level requires a margin of error of about two standard deviations. The margin of error is 2%, so 2σ must be equal to .02. This leads to the equation

$$2 \cdot \frac{.5}{\sqrt{n}} = .02$$

which gives $n = 2500$.

For Question 2, *The Normal Table* shows that a confidence level of 97% corresponds to a margin of error of approximately 2.2 standard deviations. The equation for n becomes $2.2 \cdot \frac{.5}{\sqrt{n}} = .05$, which gives $n = 484$. If students interpolate to find that a 97% confidence level corresponds more precisely to 2.17σ, they will get $n \approx 472$.

For Question 3, the margin of error is 2σ and $\sigma = \frac{.5}{\sqrt{400}}$, which gives $2\sigma = .05$. In other words, the margin of error is 5%.

For Question 4, $\sigma = \frac{.5}{\sqrt{100}}$, which equals .05. The margin of error is 3%, which is $.6\sigma$, so the confidence level (45%) is found using $z = .6$. Point out that in seeking a small margin of error with a fairly small sample size, this pollster has ended up with a very poor confidence level.

How Big?

Intent

Students select the sample size for their polling projects.

Mathematics

Students apply their knowledge about how sample size is related to confidence level and margin of error in order to determine how large a sample they want to take for their polls.

Progression

Students finalize their plans for their polling projects, and the teacher checks that their planned poll sizes are manageable. The teacher also reviews the schedule for completing the project and discusses the grading criteria.

Approximate Time

5 minutes for introduction
25 to 30 minutes for activity (at home or in class)
10 minutes for discussion

Classroom Organization

Pairs, followed by whole-class discussion

Doing the Activity

Tell students that they will now decide on their sample sizes and write up other aspects of their polling plans. They will then collect their data (that is, carry out their poll) over the next couple of days.

Discussing and Debriefing the Activity

Ask several pairs to report the sample size they have chosen and how they made their decision. If anyone has questions about their plan, elicit responses from the rest of the class.

Verify that the sample sizes are practical. If any seem unworkable, you might urge the students to rethink their goals for confidence level and margin of error.

Review with students that they will have be given time in class to analyze their poll results, write up their reports, and prepare their presentations. Therefore, they need to do their polling before that day.

If feasible, look over the rest of the information students turn in as soon as possible, in case there are any problems that you want to alert students to before they do their polling.

Finally, before students finish preparing their presentations, take some time to discuss the criteria you will use in grading these presentations.

Putting It Together

Intent

In these activities, students solve the central unit problem.

Mathematics

These activities focus on having students pull together the various concepts from this unit in order to analyze a poll or problem situation.

Progression

In *Roberto and the Coin,* students apply their new concepts to a problem from a previous unit. In *How Much Better Is Bigger?* they experiment with how poll size can affect margin of error and confidence level. Next, they turn to completing their analysis of the central unit problem in *"The Pollster's Dilemma" Revisited* and then apply all they have learned in the unit to their polling project, including *Final Data Collection*.

Roberto and the Coin
How Much Better Is Bigger?
"The Pollster's Dilemma" Revisited
Final Data Collection
"The Pollster's Dilemma" Portfolio

Roberto and the Coin

Intent

Students apply concepts from this unit to a problem from an earlier unit.

Mathematics

Students examine a familiar problem using the tools they have acquired in this unit.

Progression

Students consider whether a coin that lands on heads 573 out of 1000 flips is a fair coin. They use a normal approximation to find out how likely it would be for a fair coin to give these results and then calculate specific confidence intervals for the true probability of getting heads with this coin.

Approximate Time

35 to 45 minutes

Classroom Organization

Small groups, followed by whole-class discussion

Doing the Activity

This activity needs no introduction.

Discussing and Debriefing the Activity

Question 1a

Have one or two volunteers explain what it means that the binomial distribution can be approximated by the normal distribution. Here are the key ideas:

- The binomial distribution looks more and more like the normal distribution as the value of n (in this context, the number of coin flips) increases.
- The normal distribution that best approximates a particular binomial distribution will have the same mean and standard deviation as the binomial distribution.

- It's useful to approximate the binomial distribution with the normal distribution because it is easier to find probabilities for various ranges of results for the normal distribution than for the binomial distribution.

Comment: With increasingly powerful technology, working with the binomial distribution is becoming less difficult, so the advantages of the normal distribution may become less meaningful. However, the central limit theorem states that the normal distribution provides an approximation for the distribution of averages for *any* probability distribution. Thus, using the normal distribution for approximations will probably continue to be of value.

Question 1b

Ask students from a couple of groups to report on their work.

If students choose to focus on the *number* of heads, rather than the *proportion,* they need to remember to go back to the formulas they found in *The Search Is On!* In particular, the standard deviation is given by the expression $\sqrt{np(1-p)}$ rather than $\sqrt{\dfrac{p(1-p)}{n}}$. This gives $\sigma = \sqrt{250}$ (roughly 15.8).

This means Roberto's sampling result of 573 heads is $\dfrac{73}{\sqrt{250}}$ (roughly 4.6) standard deviations above the true proportion for a fair coin. *The Normal Table* does not show much detail for such large z-values, but it does show that the probability corresponding to $z = 4$ is .99994. Thus, the chance of being more than 4 standard deviations from the mean is less than .00006. The probability of being more than 4.6 standard deviations from the mean is actually about .000004, or roughly four in a million (and the probability of being this far *above* the mean is half of that).

Students can also do the analysis in terms of proportions rather than actual numbers of heads. In that case, $\sigma \approx .0158$ and the sample proportion is .573, compared to a mean (for a fair coin) of .5. Once again, if the coin were fair, the difference of .073 between the sample proportion and the true proportion would be roughly 4.6 times the standard deviation.

Explain that the χ^2 statistic for this situation is roughly 21.3 and that the probability of getting a χ^2 statistic this high or higher is, again, roughly .000004, the same as the value found using the normal approximation.

Question 2

For Question 2, students need to decide whether to use $\hat{p}$ (which is roughly .57) in place of p in the formula for σ or to use the worst-case value, $p = .5$. If they use both values, point out how little difference it makes. Using .57 for p gives $\sigma \approx 15.66$, while using .5 for p gives $\sigma \approx 15.81$. (Here, σ is given for the number of heads rather than the proportion.)

This means that a 95% confidence interval for the true mean of the coin is from about 542 heads to about 604 heads (using $z = 2$ and $\sigma = 15.66$). That is, one can say with 95% confidence that the probability of heads for that coin is between .542 and .604. The 99% confidence interval is from about 532 heads to about 614 heads (using $z = 2.6$ and $\sigma = 15.66$), which means a probability of heads between .532 and .614.

Question 3

Because the value of .5 is outside the 99% confidence interval, Roberto can be more than 99% confident that the coin is not fair.

This is a good occasion to review the distinction between *confidence* and *probability* (see the subsection "Confidence Versus Probability" in the discussion introducing *The Worst-Case Scenario*). It does not make sense to talk about the probability that this coin is fair—it either is or it isn't—so we instead speak of the *confidence* Roberto can have in concluding the coin is not fair.

How Much Better Is Bigger?

Intent

Students explore how confidence level increases as poll size continues to increase.

Mathematics

This activity gives students another opportunity to work with how the concepts of poll size, margin of error, and confidence level are related. Students see that beyond a certain point, increasing n does not significantly improve the confidence level.

Progression

Students select three large poll sizes and compare (1) the confidence levels that would be achieved with a 5% margin of error and (2) the margins of error that would accompany a 95% confidence level. They see that as n increases, the impact of the change in n on the margin of error gradually decreases.

Approximate Time

5 minutes for introduction
30 minutes for activity (at home or in class)
10 minutes for discussion

Classroom Organization

Individuals, followed by whole-class discussion

Doing the Activity

Take a moment to discuss with students what poll sizes they might use. Emphasize that the three sizes should be quite different. For instance, polls of size 50, 200, and 800 will be more illuminating than polls of size 210, 220, and 230.

Discussing and Debriefing the Activity

Question 1a

Let three or four students each present the confidence level they found for a different poll size.

For example, using $n = 500$, students should get $\sigma = .02236$ (using $\sigma = \dfrac{.5}{\sqrt{n}}$ based on the worst-case scenario). In this case, a 5% margin of error represents roughly 2.24 standard deviations (because $\dfrac{.05}{.02236} \approx 2.24$). *The Normal Table* shows that $z = 2.24$ corresponds to a confidence level of approximately 97.5%.

Here are the *z*-values and confidence levels corresponding to a few other poll sizes (for a 5% margin of error):

- $n = 50$: $z \approx 0.71$, confidence level $\approx$ 52.2%
- $n = 100$: $z \approx 1$, confidence level $\approx$ 68.3%
- $n = 750$: $z \approx 2.74$, confidence level $\approx$ 99.4%
- $n = 900$: $z \approx 3$, confidence level $\approx$ 99.7%

Question 1b

Students should certainly see that the confidence level rises as *n* increases. They should also see that beyond a certain point, increases in *n* lead to very little change in the confidence level.

You might ask, **Why doesn't the confidence level change much beyond a certain value of *n*?** One simple explanation is that there isn't much increase available—the confidence level can't go beyond 100%!

Another approach is to point out that there are only two possible answers to the poll—"yes" and "no"—and we shouldn't need more than, say, 500 people to determine within 5% what the whole population is like.

Question 2a

In Question 2, the confidence level is fixed and the margin of error is changing as *n* varies. Students do not need the normal table, because the 95% confidence level always corresponds to 2 standard deviations (or, more precisely, to 1.96 standard deviations). Instead, they simply need to find σ using the formula $\sigma = \dfrac{.5}{\sqrt{n}}$ and then use 2σ for the margin of error. Thus, the margin of error is $\dfrac{1}{\sqrt{n}}$, and students need only substitute their values for *n*.

Here are some sample values:

- $n = 100$: margin of error $\approx 10\%$
- $n = 500$: margin of error $\approx 4.5\%$
- $n = 750$: margin of error $\approx 3.7\%$
- $n = 900$: margin of error $\approx 3.3\%$

Question 2b

Students should see that the margin of error decreases as n increases.

They should also see that as n increases, adding a particular number of additional people to the poll leads to smaller changes in the margin of error. For instance, going from $n = 100$ to $n = 500$ (an increase of 400) decreases the margin of error from 10% to 4.5%, a substantial decrease. But going from $n = 500$ to $n = 900$ (again, an increase of 400) only decreases the margin of error from 4.5% to 3.7%.

Key Question

Why doesn't the confidence level change much beyond a certain value of n?

"The Pollster's Dilemma" Revisited

Intent

Students analyze the central unit problem using the tools developed in the unit.

Mathematics

Analyzing the unit problem requires students to synthesize concepts from throughout the unit.

Progression

Students now return to the central unit problem and answer the question, "What does this poll result mean?" The subsequent discussion focuses on the confidence Coretta can have that she really is leading.

Approximate Time

40 minutes

Classroom Organization

Individuals, followed by whole-class discussion

Doing the Activity

The unit now returns to the original situation from *The Pollster's Dilemma*. Students' discussion and write-ups for this activity can serve as a model for their written work on their project, *Let's Vote on It!*

Discussing and Debriefing the Activity

Let one or two students report on their analyses. Here is an outline of the ideas that should emerge:

- The standard deviation for a poll of size 500 is at most $\dfrac{.5}{\sqrt{500}}$ (as usual, using the worse-case scenario), or approximately .0224.
- Because the poll shows Coretta with 53% of the vote, this means she was leading at the time of the poll unless the true proportion is below the poll result by more than 3%. (If the true proportion is above the sample proportion, she's in great shape!)

- Because Coretta's "safety margin" is .03 and the standard deviation is .0224, the safety margin is approximately 1.34 standard deviations.
- According to the normal table, a z-value of 1.34 corresponds to a probability of roughly .82. Therefore, one can say with 82% confidence that the true proportion is between 50% and 56%.
- Coretta is also safe if the true proportion is above 56% (that is, in the upper tail of the distribution), so one should add half of the remaining .18 to the value of .82 to get a confidence level of .91.

Thus, Coretta can be 91% confident that she was leading in the overall population at the time of this poll.

Some students may find the margin of error for this poll using the standard 95% confidence level, even though that isn't what they were asked for. If so, they should get that the margin of error is approximately .045. In other words, the pollster can be 95% confident that the true mean lies between 48.5% and 57.5%.

Final Data Collection

Intent

Students finish collecting data for their polling project.

Mathematics

In *How Big?*, students selected a sample size and finalized their plans for the polling project described in *Let's Vote on It!* Now they conclude their data collection in preparation for analyzing the results and completing their reports.

Progression

Students use this final opportunity to collect the data for their polling project.

Approximate Time

20 to 40 minutes (at home or in class)

Classroom Organization

Individuals, followed by pairs

Doing the Activity

If needed, remind students that they need to have their polling completed for their project in time for tomorrow's class, so they can work on their reports and presentations during class.

Discussing and Debriefing the Activity

Reserve much of the class period on the following day for students to work on their projects and prepare their presentations. If time allows, you may want to allot an additional day for this work. This project seems to be where many students are finally able to bring the various concepts from the unit together effectively.

"The Pollster's Dilemma" Portfolio

Intent

Students reflect upon the unit's key concepts as they compile their unit portfolios and write their cover letters.

Mathematics

The portfolio asks students to summarize the main mathematical ideas from the unit and how they were developed and applied to the unit problem. When selecting papers for inclusion with the cover letter, they are asked to focus on activities involving standard deviation as well as those that demonstrate the relationship between confidence interval, margin of error, and poll size.

Progression

Students select activities for inclusion in their unit portfolios and write their cover letters summarizing the unit.

Approximate Time

30 to 40 minutes for activity (at home or in class)
10 to 15 minutes for discussion

Classroom Organization

Individuals, followed by whole-class discussion

Doing the Activity

Have students read the instructions in the student book carefully.

Discussing and Debriefing the Activity

You may want to have students share their cover letters as a way to start a summary discussion of the unit. Then let them brainstorm ideas of what they have learned in this unit. This is a good opportunity to review terminology and to place this unit in a broader mathematics context.

Blackline Masters

Sampling Seniors

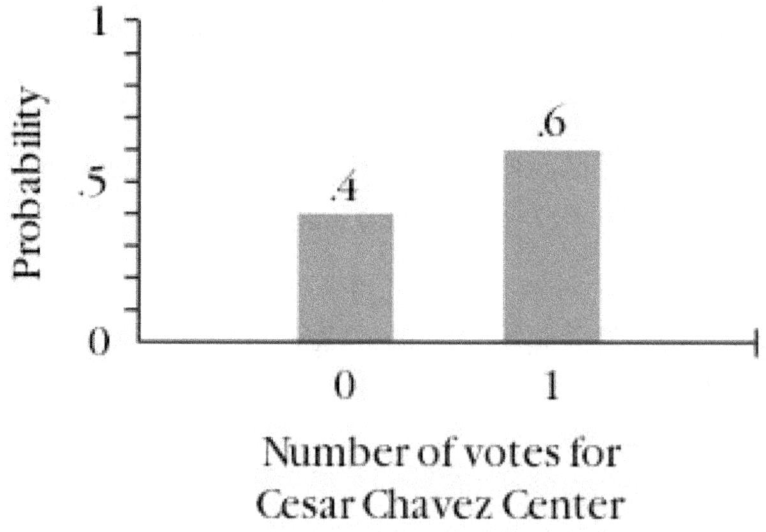

Probability
1
.5
0
.4
.6
0
1
Number of votes for
Cesar Chavez Center

Distribution of 3-person polls with
true proportion = 60%

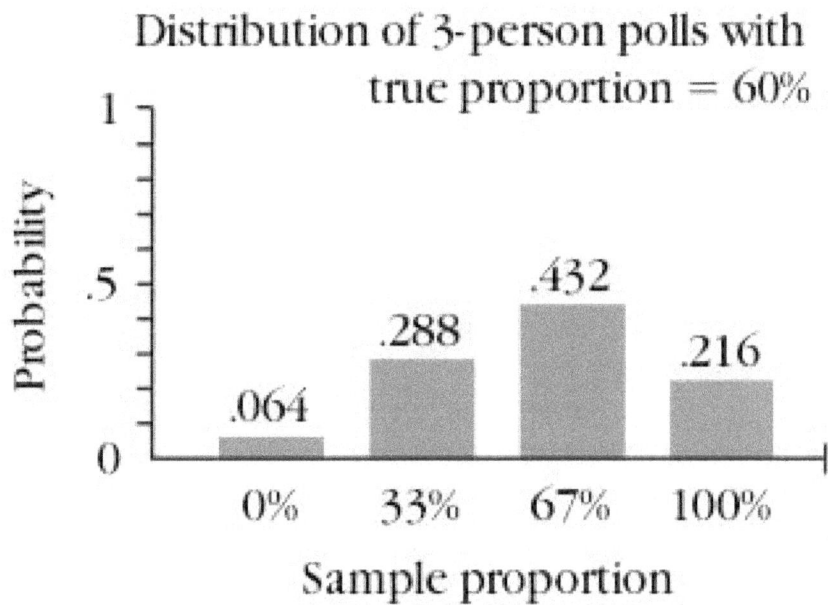

Distribution of 3-person polls with true proportion = 55%

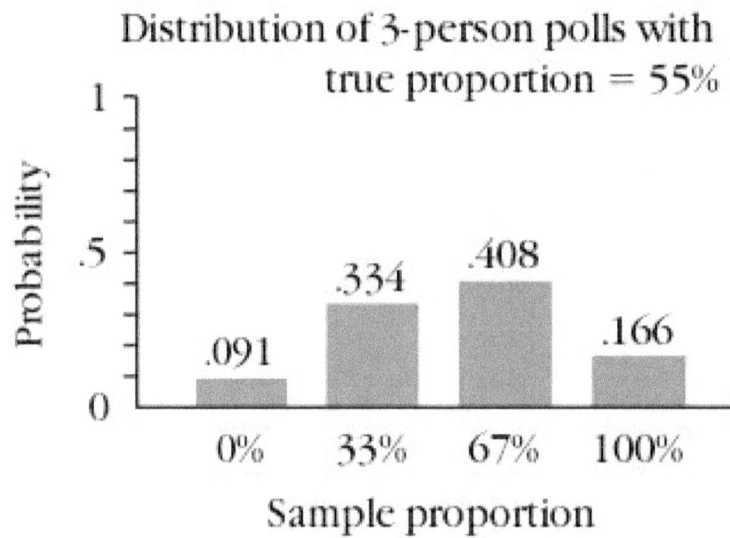

Distribution of 3-person polls with
true proportion = 70%

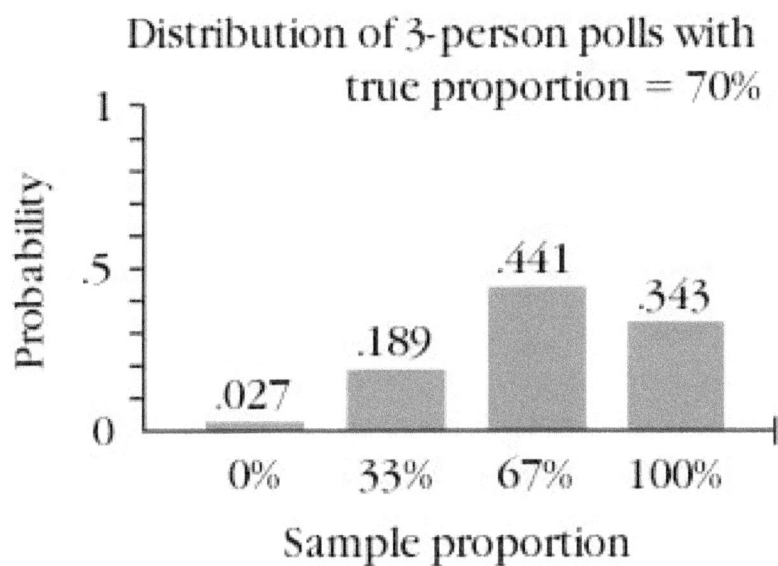

Distribution of 5-person polls with true proportion = 60%

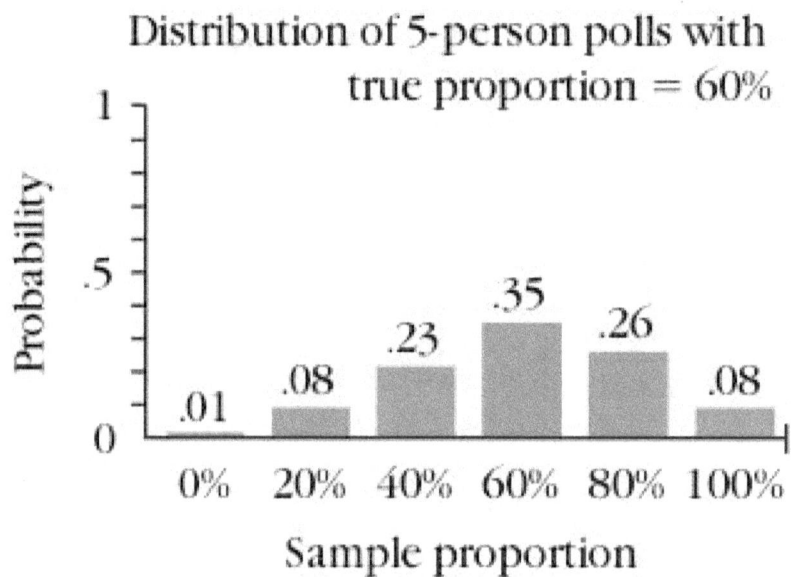

Distribution of 9-person polls with
true proportion = 60%

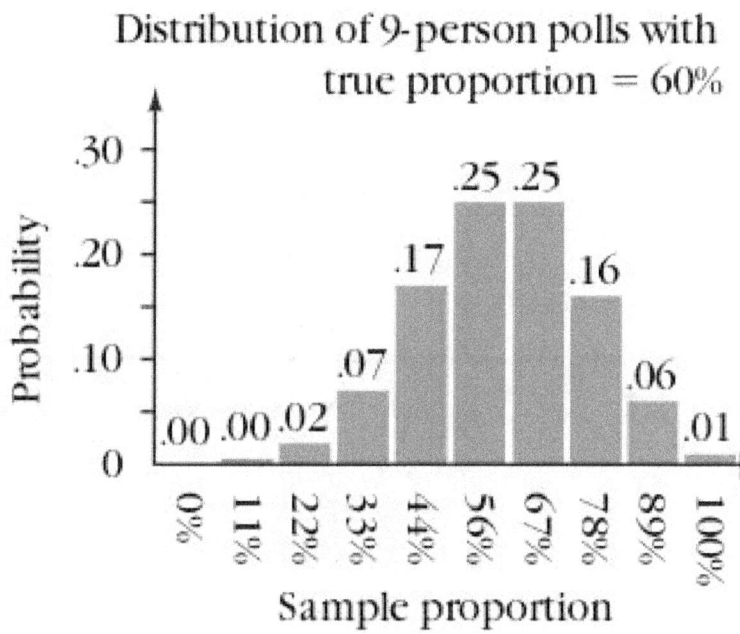

Distribution of 50-person polls with
true proportion = 60%

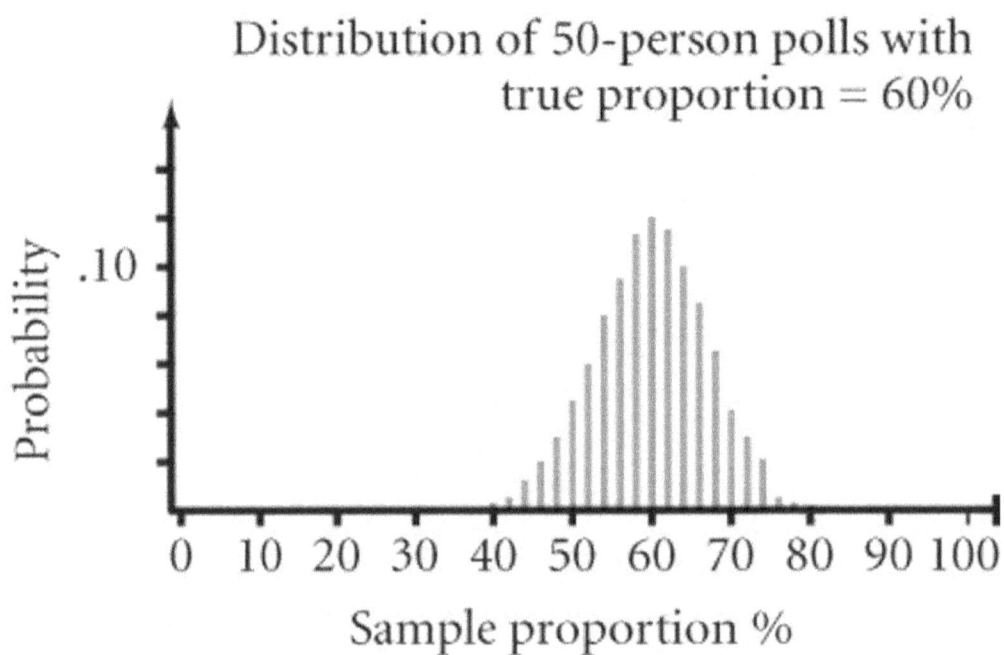

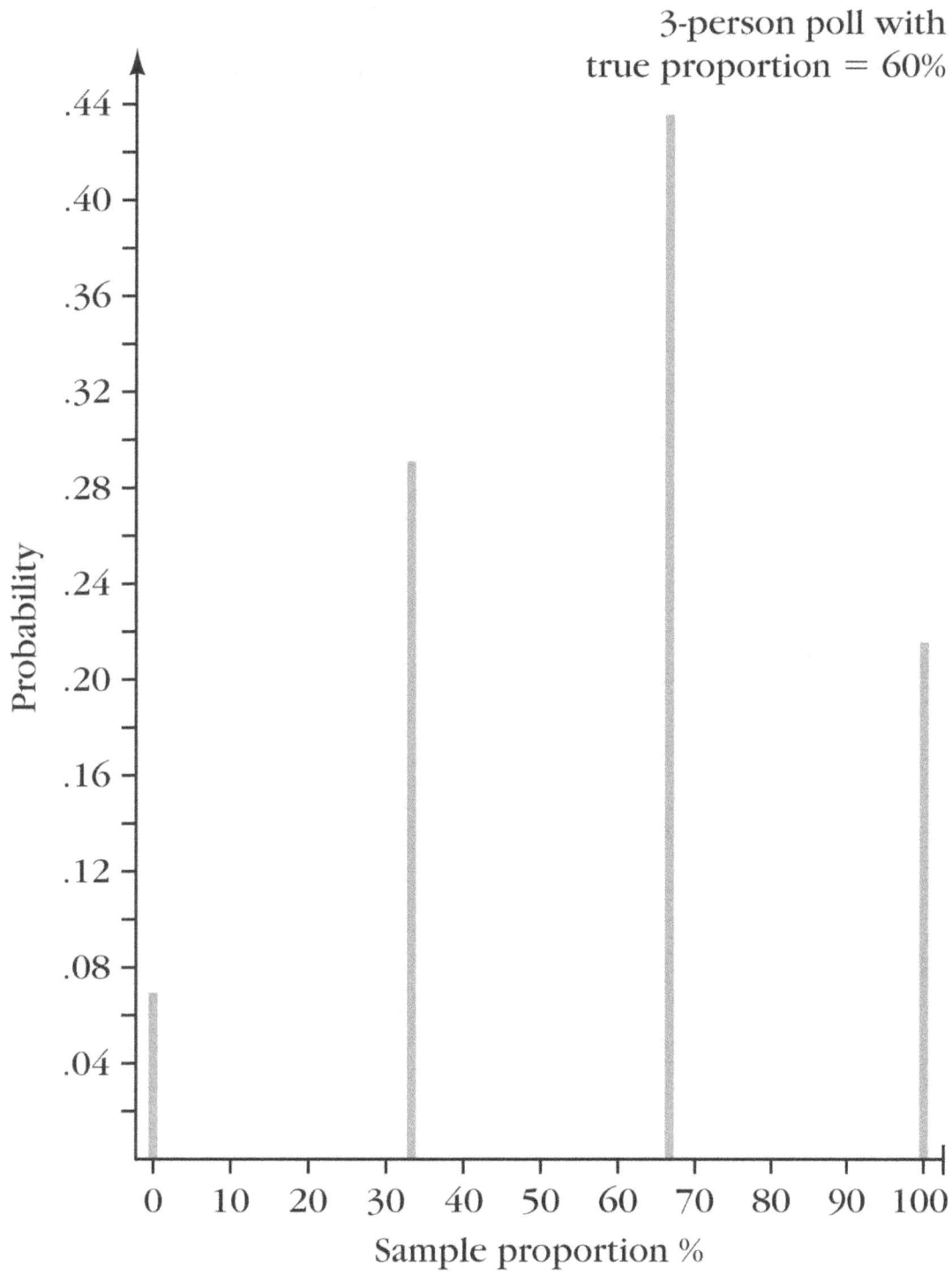

3-person poll with true proportion = 60%

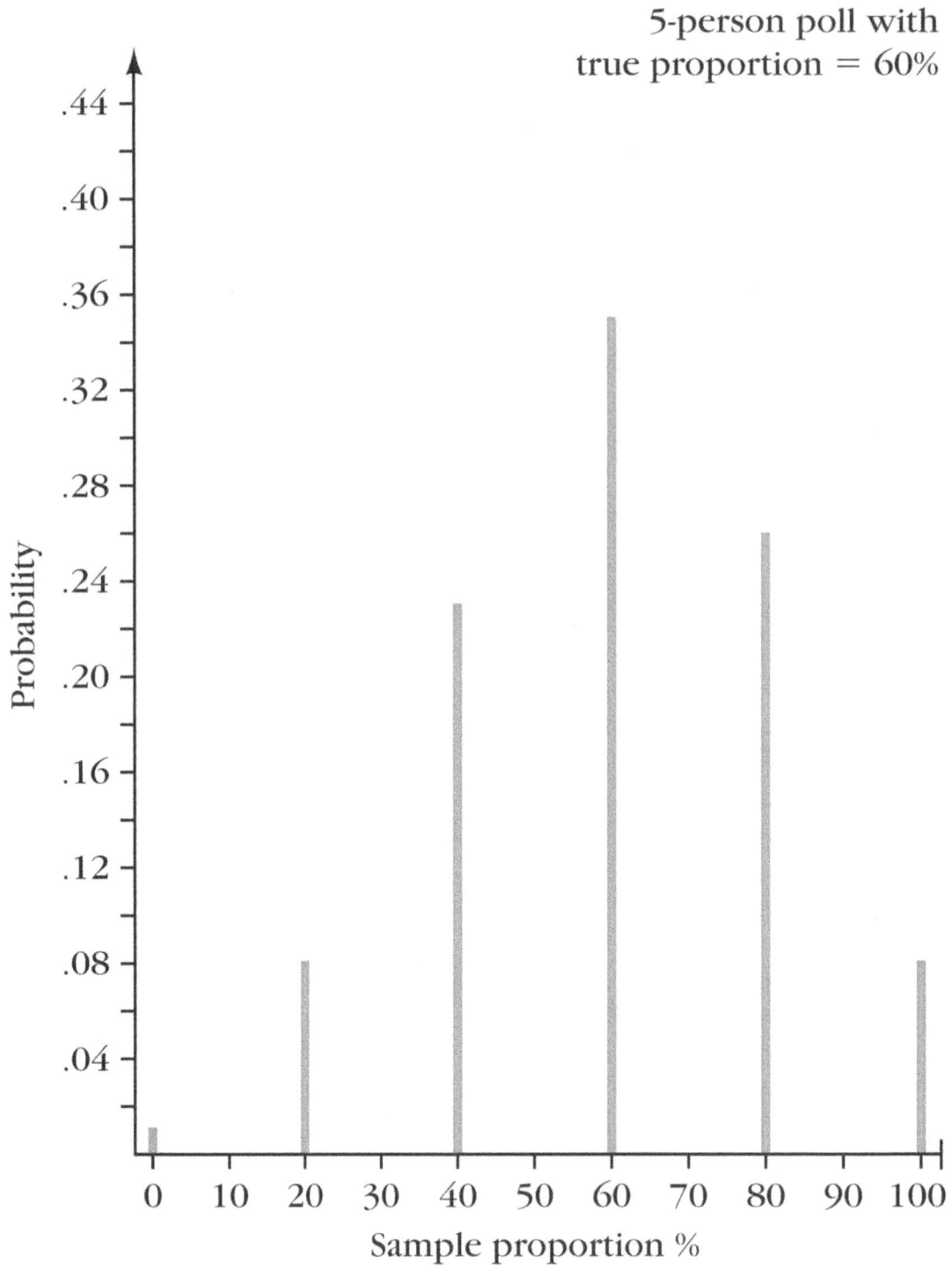

5-person poll with true proportion = 60%

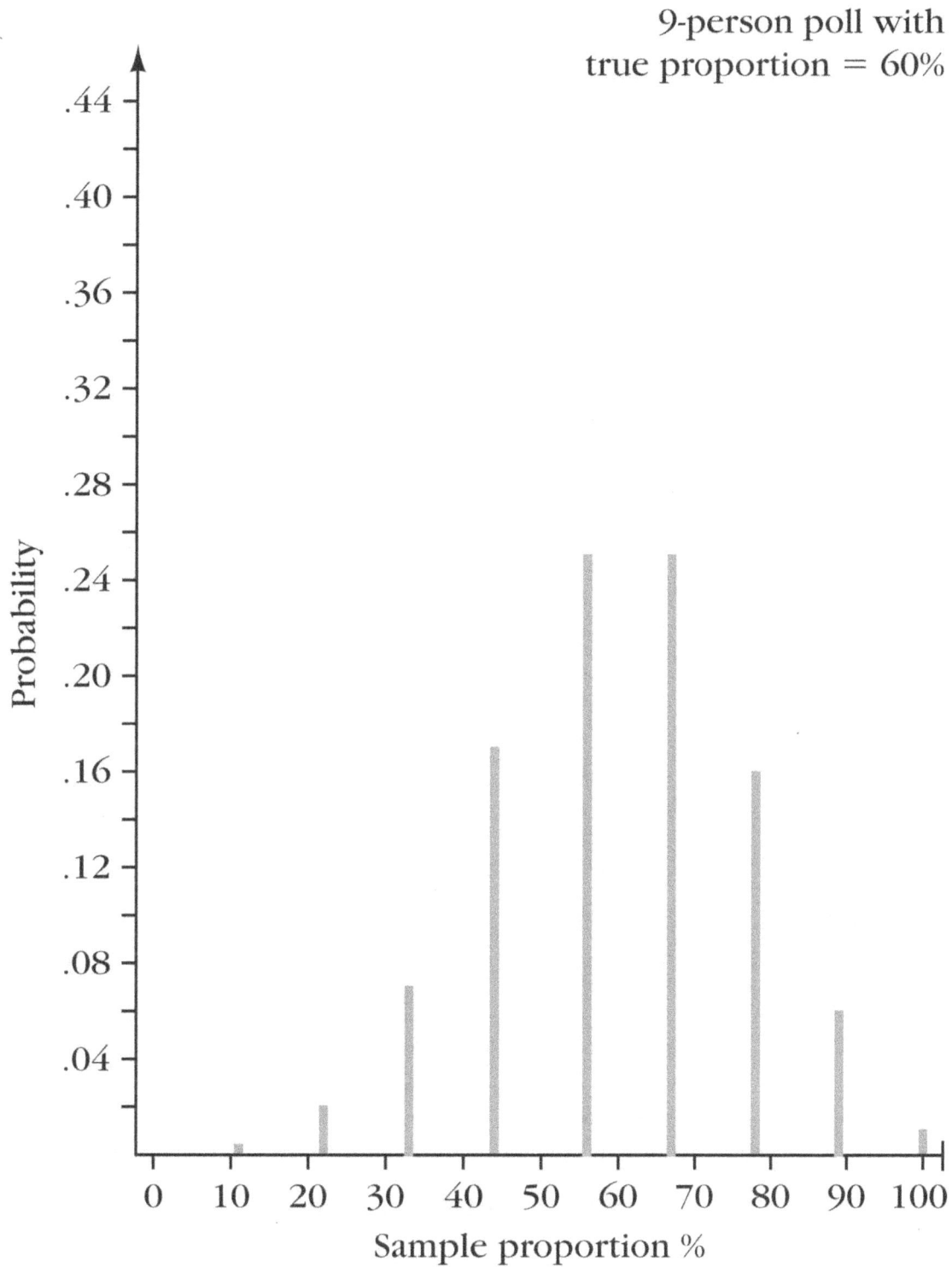

9-person poll with
true proportion = 60%

50-person poll with
true proportion = 60%

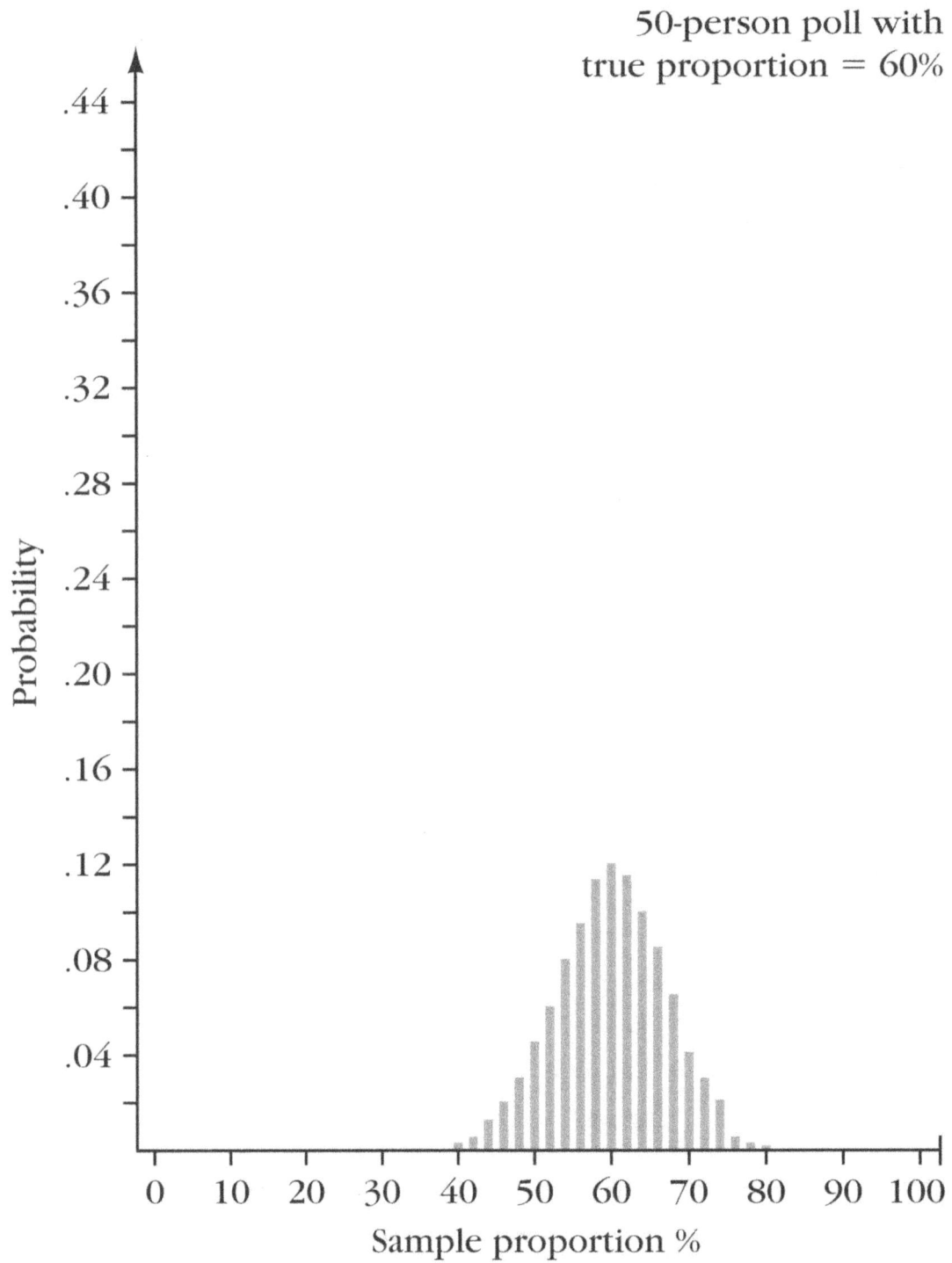

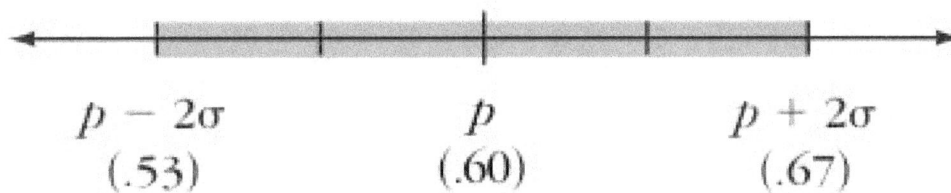

$p - 2\sigma$ (.53) p (.60) $p + 2\sigma$ (.67)

$\hat{p}$ will fall within the shaded region

approximately 95% of the time.

$$\widehat{p} - 2\sigma \qquad\qquad \underset{(.581)}{\widehat{p}} \qquad\qquad \widehat{p} + 2\sigma$$

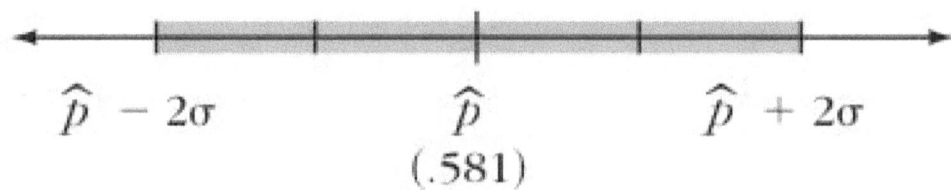

**The shaded region will include *p*
approximately 95% of the time.**

¼-Inch Graph Paper

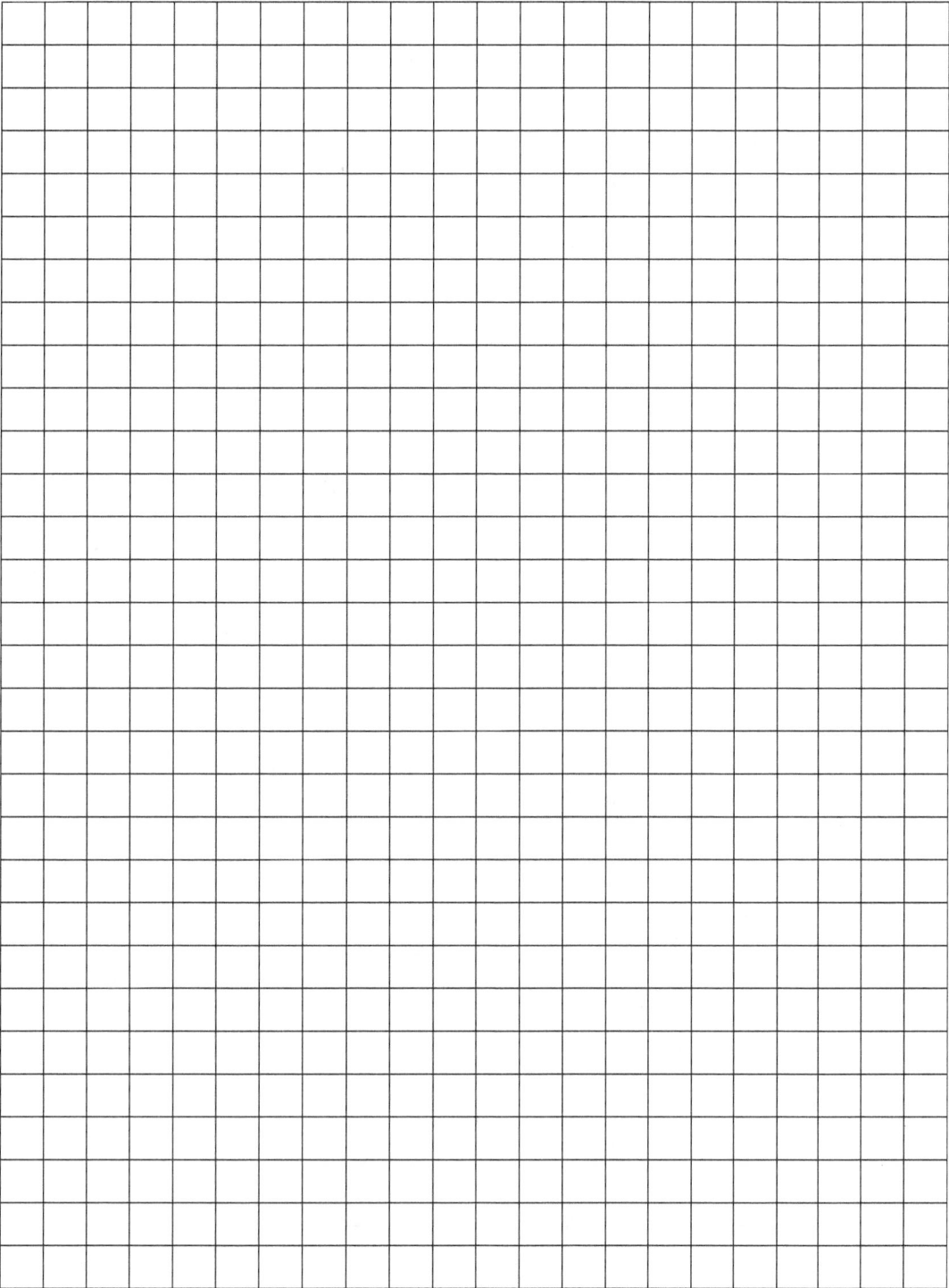

1-Centimeter Graph Paper

1-Inch Graph Paper

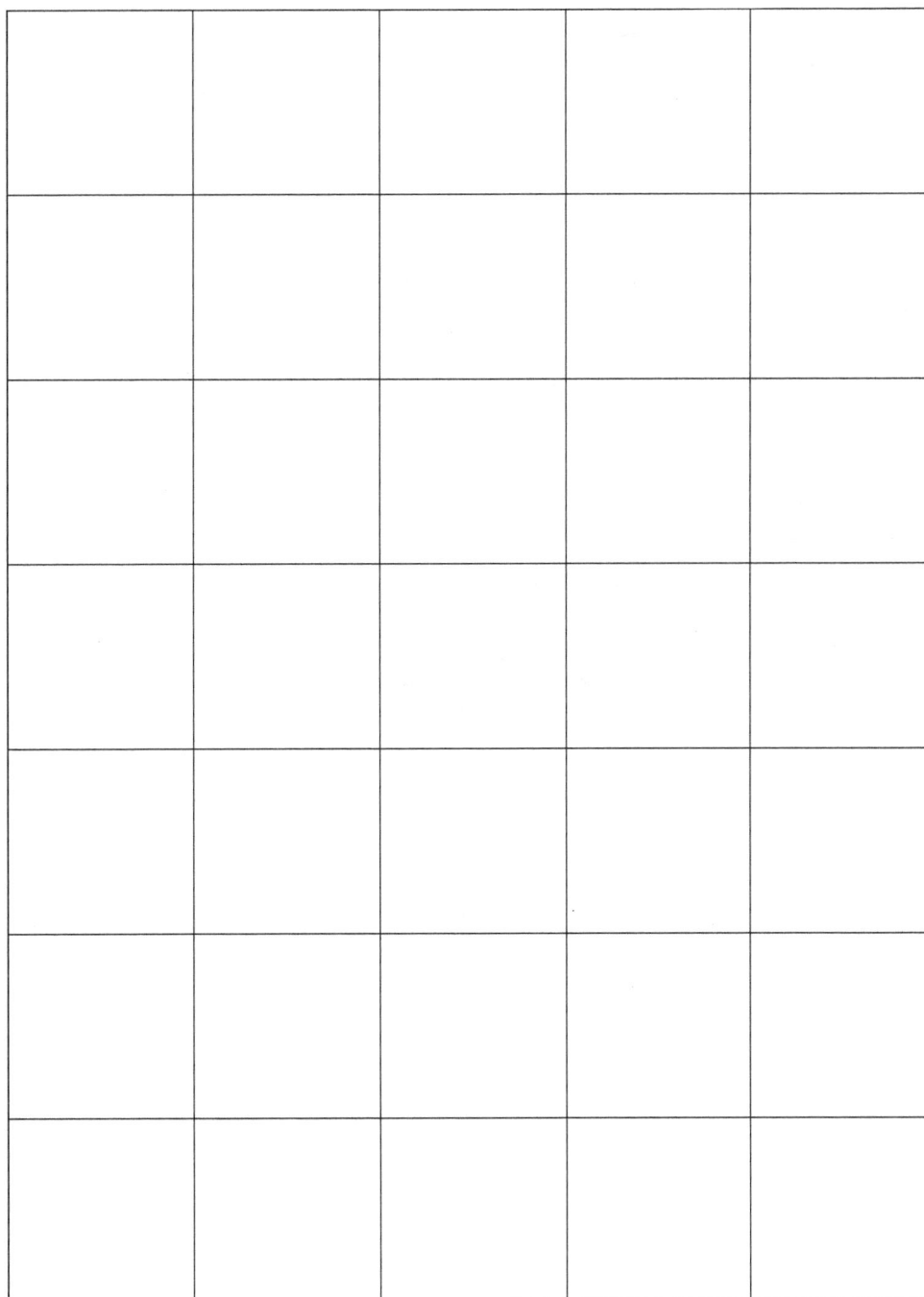

Assessments

In-Class Assessment

1. Senator Back Boneless will not make a decision on any issue unless a poll on the issue is done beforehand. He insists on knowing that a majority of his constituents want him to vote a certain way before he will vote at all. More than that, he requires that the poll have at least a 95% confidence level with at most a 4% margin of error.

   Senator Boneless has been asked to change the wallpaper in his office to plaid. How many people must he poll in order to get a result he will accept? Explain your answer.

2. If polls are taken in a two-person election from a given population, several features of the distribution of possible outcomes are related.

   a. Suppose the sample size (the number of people polled) increases. How does this affect the standard deviation of the sample proportion? Explain your answer both intuitively and in terms of appropriate formulas.

   b. Suppose the poll size is kept fixed, but the pollster chooses to set a higher confidence level. How does this affect the margin of error? Explain your answer both intuitively and in terms of the procedure for finding the margin of error.

Take-Home Assessment

1. Make a probability bar graph showing the distribution of results for a 5-person poll taken from a population in which 80% favor a certain candidate. Assume there are only two choices in the poll.

2. Coretta's most recent poll shows 160 voters for her and 140 against. What can you conclude from this poll? Give as complete an answer as you can, telling everything you know about the situation. Justify your conclusions.

I. The Diver Returns

1. Mike plays the tuba. His college's marching band is performing at halftime. At one point in the performance, the band members form a 100-foot-diameter circle in the center of the field. As the band begins to march around the circle, Mike is at the end of the circle closest to the goal line, which is 100 feet away. How far from the same goal line will he be after he has marched 320 degrees around the circle?

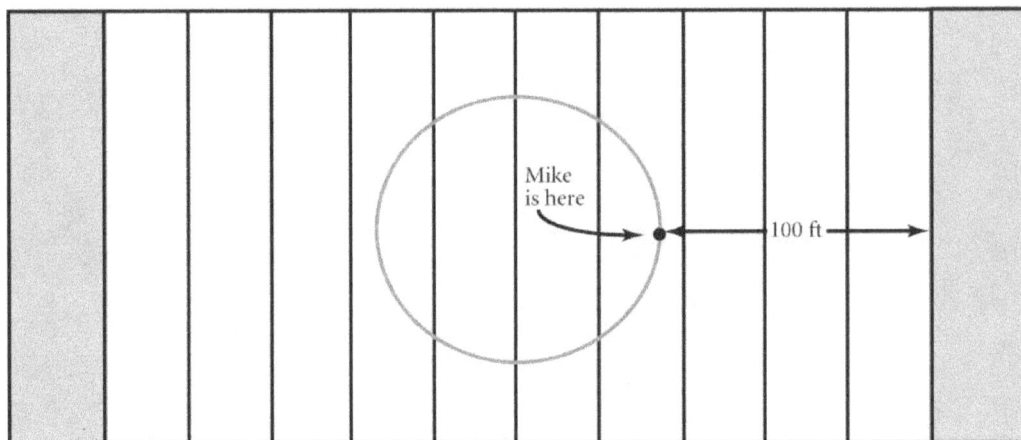

2. A coin is thrown downward with an initial velocity of 5 feet per second at an angle of 37° below the horizontal.

   a. How far will the coin move horizontally in the first 3 seconds?

   b. How far will the coin fall vertically in the first 3 seconds?

II. The World of Functions

1. a. Sketch the graph of a function that has both of these properties:

      - As x becomes very large in the positive direction, y becomes very large in the positive direction.
      - As x becomes very large in the negative direction, the graph has the x-axis as an asymptote.

    b. What is a possible algebraic equation that describes a graph like this? Explain.

2. The table shows the outputs for a function f for a given set of input values.

x	$f(x)$
−3	3
−2	0
−1	−1
0	0
1	3
2	8
3	15

    a. Plot the points represented by this table.

    b. Decide what family you think the function belongs to, and explain your reasoning.

    c. Find an algebraic expression for f that fits the information in the table.

III. The Pollster's Dilemma

1. You are one of two candidates running for office. Eighty percent of the population plans to vote for you. Of course, being humble, you have no idea that 0.8 is the true proportion. Though everyone keeps telling you that you will win, you don't quite believe it.

    When a 7-person poll is conducted, you say that you will eat your hat if five or more of the respondents plan to vote for you. What is the probability that you will be glad you have a very small hat size—that is, that five or more will say they plan to vote for you?

2. A driver's license test has a mean score of 63 with a standard deviation of 15. If 75 is the minimal passing score, about what percentage of people who take the test will pass?

The Pollster's Dilemma Calculator Guide for the TI-83/84 Family of Calculators

The Pollster's Dilemma introduces several new calculator techniques and revisits many that were introduced previously. The unit makes heavy use of the calculator's capabilities, as do most of the other Year 4 units.

Combinatorial coefficients are reviewed early in the unit. This guide then presents an optional introduction to creating bar graphs on the calculator. The technique for entering a complicated function into the calculator, first used for the *High Dive* unit problem, proves to be helpful when students graph several variations of the normal curve. In this context, this guide provides an introduction to the calculator's ability to store and recall graph databases.

Probabilities associated with the areas of regions beneath the normal curve are initially calculated using numerical integration on a calculator graph. After the normal table is introduced, we present the more flexible normal distribution probability features of the calculator, which are useful in many situations. Finally, we briefly revisit using the calculator to compute standard deviation and to find the maximum of a graphed function.

"Pennant Fever" Reflection: Some students may have used their calculators to find the combinatorial coefficient $_7C_4$ for Question 4 of *Pennant Fever Reflection*. $_nP_r$ and $_nC_r$ are found on the **PRB** menu after pressing the MATH key. The screen shown here illustrates the use of $_nC_r$ for this assignment.

```
(7 nCr 4)*.62^4*
.38^3
            .2837824881
```

The factorial function is also located on the MATH **PRB** menu.

The Theory of Polls: The probability bar graphs used throughout this unit can be generated on the calculator. The Calculator Note "Probability Bar Graphs" will probably be more useful to the teacher who wishes to display a bar graph with the overhead projection calculator than to students. There are enough pitfalls inherent in constructing the graphs on the calculator that the process can be somewhat cumbersome until you have practiced it several times.

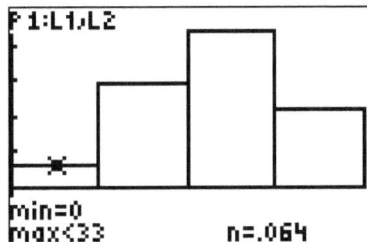

```
P1:L1,L2



min=0
max<33       n=.064
```

Graphing Distributions: The normal curve function from this activity is most easily entered into the calculator using the technique described in the Calculator Note "Graphing a Complicated Function," provided in the Calculator Notes for the Year 3 Unit *High Dive*. You might note that this technique is similar to the concept of composition.

Notice that e^x is the 2ND function of the LN key.

This activity will require students to change the values for the mean and standard deviation within their function several times. Thus, you might suggest that they make these values **Y₁** and **Y₂** and then build the rest of the function using **Y₃** and beyond. You may need to remind students that they insert the **Y** variables into their functions by selecting them from the variables menu. Press VARS, use the right arrow to display the **Y-VARS** menu, press ENTER to select **Function**, and then highlight the desired variable and press ENTER.

Remind students as well to turn off the display of the graphs for all functions except their final one. They can do this by moving the cursor to the equal sign on the Y= screen and pressing ENTER.

One possible way to enter the function for Question 1 of *Graphing Distributions* is shown here, using **Y₁** for the mean and **Y₂** for the standard deviation. For the remaining questions, you need only change the values entered at **Y₁** and **Y₂** and adjust the viewing window.

```
Plot1 Plot2 Plot3
\Y₁=0
\Y₂=1
\Y₃=1/(Y₂√(2π))
\Y₄=(X-Y₁)/Y₂
\Y₅=-.5Y₄²
\Y₆▪Y₃*e^(Y₅)
\Y₇=
```

It is useful to give students a viewing window for Question 1 and then let them adjust it for the remaining questions. A good window with which to begin has *x*-values from −4 to 4 and *y*-values from 0 to 0.4.

Because students will be using this function again in subsequent assignments and it is quite time-consuming to enter, this is a good time to introduce the calculator's ability to store a graph database. This enables students to use a single command to recall the entire list of functions, the display status of each function, and the window settings for the graph. Instructions are given in the Calculator Note "Storing and Recalling a Graph Database."

Normal Areas: The Calculator Note "Numerical Integration Under the Normal Curve" gives instructions for performing numerical integration (finding the area between a curve and the *x*-axis) with the calculator and for using the probability distribution features of the calculator. Caution students that they need to learn to use the normal distribution table as well, and that they will often find the table easier to use than the calculator's built-in features. If they learn to use both well, they can decide which will work best for a given problem.

∫f(x)dx=.9788414

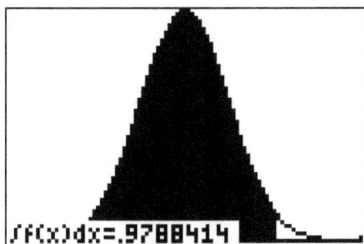

More Middletown Musings: Question 3 of this activity illustrates the power of the calculator's **normalcdf** feature, explained in the Calculator Note "Normal Distribution Probabilities on the Calculator." Several things complicate this problem when using the normal distribution table: a ratio that does not yield a friendly decimal value, a z-value that requires interpolation on the table, an asymmetrical region, and looking for the tail from that region. Notice in the screen shown here how easily the calculator avoids each of these difficulties. The value .762 represents all runners who run up to 40 miles per week. The value .237 represents those who run 40 miles per week or more. A slightly more accurate answer could be found by using a more negative lower limit, but virtually all of the data are contained within four standard deviations of the mean.

```
normalcdf(-4,5/7
)
        .7624431264
1-Ans
        .2375568736
```

Back to the Circus: This activity reveals the usefulness of the **invNorm** feature, also explained in the Calculator Note "Normal Distribution Probabilities on the Calculator."

```
invNorm(.95)
        1.644853626
Ans*.3+2
        2.493456088
```

Gaps in the Table: If you have budding programmers in the class, you might suggest that they write a calculator program that will accomplish linear interpolation, as introduced in *Gaps in the Table*.

A Normal Poll: The calculator solution to Question 2 is shown here. As noted earlier, the upper limit of 4 can be used in place of infinity, because very little data will be found more than four standard deviations above the mean.

```
normalcdf(-.1/.0
69,4)
         .9263379237
```

The Search Is On!: As discussed with *Pennant Feature Reflection,* the combinatorial coefficients needed for this activity are located on the MATH **PRB** menu.

From Numbers to Proportions: This activity can be most easily approached by having the calculator find the mean and standard deviation. The Calculator Note "Standard Deviation with the Calculator" gives instructions. This feature was introduced in the Year 1 unit *The Pit and the Pendulum.*

Once the data set for Question 1 has been entered into **List 1** and the statistics for that data set have been calculated, show your students the following shortcut for completing Question 2. Find the proportions of votes for all of the six results from **List 1** at once by pressing 2ND [L1] ÷ 5 0 0 STO> 2ND [L2]. (**L₁** and **L₂** are located above the 1 and 2 keys.) This stores the proportions in List 2. Now simply tell the calculator to find the one-variable statistics for List 2, as shown here.

```
L₁/500→L₂
{.48 .5 .476 .4…
1-Var Stats L₂
```

The Worst-Case Scenario: If students use a calculator graph to solve Question 1, they can find the maximum value more exactly by using the **maximum** feature from the 2ND [CALC] menu than by using the TRACE feature. Instructions for using the maximum feature are found in the Calculator Note, "Solving *Sand Castles* with the CALC Menu," provided in the Calculator Notes for the Year 3 Unit *High Dive.*

```
Plot1 Plot2 Plot3
\Y₁■√(X(1-X)/500
)
\Y₂=
\Y₃=
\Y₄=
\Y₅=
\Y₆=
```
```
Maximum
X=.49999904 _Y=.02236068
```

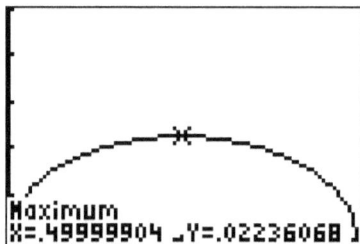

Roberto and the Coin: Question 1b involves a region of the normal table where not much detail is given by the table. Even a rough interpolation reveals that there is an extremely small probability that we will get a result like this if the coin is fair. But it is interesting to pursue a more exact solution to see just how small that probability is. The accuracy of the answer will be affected both by the place to which the *z*-value is rounded and by the limitations of interpolation. This is a good problem to explore using the calculator's built-in distribution features. The solution is shown in the screen.

```
73/√(250)
          4.616925384
normalcdf( -Ans,A
ns)
          .9999961012
1-Ans
      3.89878642E-6
```

Probability Bar Graphs

These instructions explain how to construct probability bar graphs. They use as an example the probability distribution of 3-person polls with a true proportion of 60%, as discussed in *The Theory of Polls* and summarized in the table here.

Sample proportion	Probability
0%	0.064
35%	0.288
67%	0.432
100%	0.216

1. Press STAT, and then press ENTER to select **Edit**. Clear any existing data items from the lists **L1** and **L2** by moving the cursor onto each of the two column headings and pressing CLEAR ENTER. Enter the data items from the left side of the table into the list under the **L1** heading and the data items from the right side of the table into the list under the **L2** heading. These instructions assume that the percentage values are entered in List 1 as integers between 0 and 100. (If you wish to construct a bar graph from an unsorted data set, such as a list of results from an experiment, put all of the data items into L1. The order is not important.)

2. To turn on the bar graph mode, press 2ND [STAT PLOT] and then press ENTER to select **Plot1**. Press ENTER to select **On**. Move the cursor to the bar graph symbol and press ENTER to select it.

3. Select **L1** as the source for **Xlist**. Move the cursor to the right of **Xlist** and then press 2ND [L1] (located above the 1 key). (If **L1** contains a list of data items for which the frequencies have not been counted, select **1** as the frequency. The calculator will determine how many pieces of data fall within the range for each bar of the graph.)

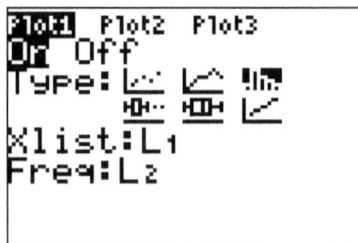

4. Press WINDOW to set up the viewing window and the scale for the graph.

a. Set **Xmin** equal to the low end of the range of values that will be represented on the graph. In this example, it will be zero.

b. The next step requires some careful thought. **Xmax** will determine the right-hand edge of the viewing window, and **Xscl** will define the width of each bar. In our example, the values for the bars, if not rounded, are actually $33\frac{1}{3}$% apart. Because the data items for the second bar were rounded downward to 33%, using a value of 33.3 for **Xscl** would cause the 33% data items to be improperly combined with those in the first bar, because the second bar would only contain values greater than 33.3. (Data items falling exactly at the division between bars will be placed in the bar to the right.) If you instead use a value of 33 for **Xscl**, the 0% data items will correctly fall in the 0-to-33 bar, the 33% items in the 33-to-66 bar, the 67% items in the 66-to-99 bar, and the 100% items in a 99-to-132 bar. This means that if you set **Xmax** at 100, nearly all of the bar containing the 100% data items will be invisible off the right-hand edge of the screen. For this reason, **Xmax** must be set at 132, even though data values greater than 100 are not possible. **Ymin** will be zero, and **Ymax** must be large enough to contain the largest frequency (probability) from the table.

5. Press GRAPH to view the graph. Press TRACE and use the right and left arrows to view the frequency and range values for each bar. If the display of these values hides the bottom of your graph, change **Ymin** to a small negative value in order to raise the graph on the screen. The calculator will correctly display the upper end of the range for each bar with a < symbol.

Storing and Recalling a Graph Database

These instructions describe how to store and recall a graph database. This feature can help you to avoid the need to repeatedly enter complicated functions into your calculator by storing them for future recall. A single command will allow you to store or recall this information:

- All functions in the Y= screen and the display status of each
- The graphing mode
- All viewing window variables
- Format settings
- The line style for each Y= function

To store a graph database (GDB) press 2ND [DRAW], use the right arrow to display the **STO** menu, and press 3 to select **StoreGDB.** The **StoreGDB** command will be copied to the home screen. Press any number key to select one of ten variables to which this GDB can be stored, and then press ENTER. To select a variable name, press VARS, press 3 to select **GDB**, press the number key to select the desired variable, and then press ENTER.

```
StoreGDB 2
            Done
```

Use the same procedure to recall the stored GDB, but select **RecallGDB** from the 2ND [DRAW] **STO** menu instead of **StoreGDB.** Again, enter the variable number from which you wish to recall the GDB and press ENTER.

Caution: Recalling the GDB replaces all Y= functions. Any functions that are entered at the Y= screen will be erased when the GDB is recalled.

Numerical Integration Under the Normal Curve

Integration refers to the process of finding the area under a curve between two *x*-values. Your calculator can arrive at a very close approximation of such areas using a process known as numerical integration.

Note: A major topic in calculus is showing that there is a close relationship between integration and differentiation (that is, finding derivatives). Based on this relationship, you can use algebraic techniques to get exact expressions for areas under some curves. But that approach doesn't work for the area under a normal curve, and numerical integration is needed.

As an example, let's use numerical integration to find the probability that a result is within two standard deviations of the mean. (You already know that this value should be about 95%, so it makes a nice illustration of the procedure.)

1. Enter the equation for a standard normal curve as given in the activity *Normal Areas*. (If you previously stored this equation as a graph database, simply recall the GDB now.) Use a mean of 0 and a standard deviation of 1 in your function. Adjust the viewing window as necessary to obtain a display of the graph of the standard normal curve.

    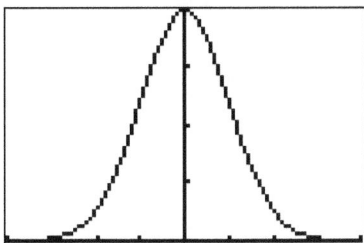

2. Press 2ND [CALC] and then press 7 to select ∫f(x)dx. (This notation means the integral of a function of *x* with respect to *x*.)

    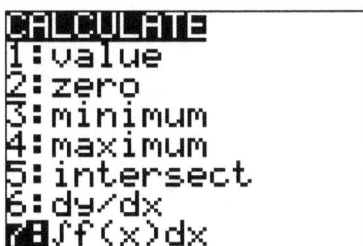

3. The calculator will request that you define a lower limit for the integration. Because you want to integrate for the region within two standard deviations of the mean, your lower limit for this example will be −2 and your upper limit will be 2. To set the lower limit, simply use the keys to enter **-2** and press ENTER.

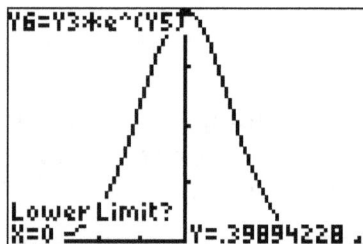

4. Select the upper limit (2, in this example) in the same manner.

5. When you press ENTER after selecting the upper limit, the calculator will shade the region between the limits and then will report the area of the shaded region. Compare this value to the value that the normal table gives for a *z*-value of 2.0.

Note: If you wish to perform another integration, it will be necessary to erase the current graph using the **ClrDraw** command from the 2ND [DRAW] menu.

Normal Distribution Probabilities on the Calculator

The calculator has several built-in features that are related to distributions, including two related to normal distributions that will be useful in this unit.

Cumulative Probability

The calculator has a cumulative probability feature that works very much like a built-in normal table. Press 2ND [DISTR] (above the VARS key) and then press 2 to select **normalcdf**. (Don't confuse this with the first menu entry, **normalpdf**, which you will not use in this unit. **normalpdf** computes the probability density function for the normal distribution. **normalcdf** computes the probability within a given interval.) The command **normalcdf** will be pasted to the home screen. Following this command, enter the left and right boundaries of the region for which you want to know the probability. Just like with the normal table, these values are numbers of standard deviations from the mean (z-values). For example, to calculate the probability that a result is within two standard deviations of the mean, use a range of −2 to 2, as shown here.

```
DISTR DRAW          normalcdf(-2,2)
1:normalpdf(                .954499876
2:normalcdf(
3:invNorm(
4:invT(
5:tpdf(
6:tcdf(
7↓X²pdf(
```

There are two major advantages of this calculator feature over the printed normal table. You can accurately find values that fall between the values given in the table, and you are not limited to working with regions that are symmetrical about the mean.

For example, consider the area of the one-tail region under the normal curve bounded by −∞ on the left and by $z = 1$ on the right. Using the table from the student text, it is necessary to find the area between $z = -1$ and $z = 1$, approximately 68%, and then add half of the remaining 32% to account for the left-hand tail. This is accomplished easily by entering **normalcdf(-4,1)**. Notice that because very few data items fall more than four standard deviations from the mean, you get an excellent approximation by using −4 in place of −∞.

```
normalcdf(-4,1)
        .8413130544
```

Inverse Normal

The calculator also has an inverse normal feature that allows you to input a probability and get the upper limit for the distribution that has that probability. This is almost like using the normal table in the reverse direction, with one important distinction. The inverse normal feature does not assume a region that is symmetrical about the mean, but assumes a region that has a lower limit of $-\infty$.

For example, suppose you want to know the region that corresponds to a probability of 97.5%. Press 2ND [DISTR] and then press 3 to select **invNorm**. Enter the probability of .975 and press ENTER. The calculator will respond that the upper limit of this region is approximately 1.96 standard deviations above the mean. That is, there is a 97.5% probability that a result falls within a region from $-\infty$ below the mean to approximately 1.96 standard deviations above the mean.

```
invNorm(.975)
           1.959963986
```

Notice that this is not the same result you get by looking up .975 in the normal table, because that table gives you regions that are symmetrical about the mean, rather than regions that include the left-hand tail. (Note that in many statistics books, tables are set up to include the left-hand tail.)

If you want to find a region that is symmetrical about the mean and that represents a probability of 97.5%, you need to recognize that the left-hand tail for that region would contain half of the missing 2.5%, so adding in this tail gives a probability of 98.75%. If you find **invNorm(.9875)**, you get approximately 2.24, which means that the symmetrical region representing a probability of 97.5% goes from -2.24 to 2.24.

Standard Deviation with the Calculator

These instructions present a brief review of the procedures for calculating the standard deviation of a data set using the calculator.

1. Press STAT to bring up the menu for entering data items. Press ENTER to select **Edit**. If there are currently data items in List 1, use the up arrow to move the cursor onto the **L₁** heading at the top of the screen, as shown here. Press CLEAR ENTER to clear List 1. You do not need to clear any data items in other lists, because only List 1 will be used for this calculation.

L1	L2	L3	1
0	.091	------	
33	.334		
67	.408		
100	.166		
------	------		

    L1 ={0,33,67,100}

2. The data set will be entered into List 1. Move the cursor to the line below the **L₁** heading and enter each data element. After each entry, press ENTER.

3. To calculate the standard deviation of your data set, press STAT and use the right arrow key to display the CALC menu. Press ENTER to select **1-Var Stats**, and the command will be pasted to your home screen. Press 2ND [L1] after the command to specify that you want to calculate statistics for the data set in List 1. Press ENTER to display the statistics.

    1-Var Stats L₁

A number of values will be displayed. Those of most interest at this time include these:

> $\overline{x}$: the mean of the data set
>
> σx: the standard deviation
>
> n: the number of items in the data set

Note: If you are calculating the standard deviation for a second data set, after you enter the second data set and select **1-Var Stats**, a screen will appear that seems to contain the statistics for the new data set. But if you have not yet pressed ENTER, these statistics will be those from the previous data set. Your new **1-Var Stats** command is at the bottom of the screen waiting to be executed, as shown here.

```
1-Var Stats
 x̄=50
 Σx=200
 Σx²=15578
 Sx=43.11998763
 σx=37.3430047
↓n=4
1-Var Stats
```

www.ingramcontent.com/pod-product-compliance
Lightning Source LLC
LaVergne TN
LVHW081316060426

835509LV00015B/1532